Building a
Reality-Based Relationship

Building a Reality-Based Relationship

The Six Stages of Modern Marriage

Liberty Kovacs, PhD, MFT

iUniverse, Inc.
New York Lincoln Shanghai

Building a Reality-Based Relationship
The Six Stages of Modern Marriage

iUniverse books may be ordered through booksellers or by contacting:

iUniverse
2021 Pine Lake Road, Suite 100
Lincoln, NE 68512
www.iuniverse.com
1-800-Authors (1-800-288-4677)

ISBN: 978-0-595-40709-5 (pbk)
ISBN: 978-0-595-85075-4 (ebk)

Printed in the United States of America

I dedicate this book to the hundreds of clients who came to me with their concerns over the past 40 years. They shared their lives with me as a nurse psychotherapist and as a marriage and family therapist. And I can say both gratefully and honestly, that I learned as much from you as you may have learned from me.

I wish to express my deep gratitude to Allison Shaw for her excellent work in editing my work and for the friendship that evolved as a result of working so closely together.

Contents

Love and Other Difficulties

Marriage is not a ritual or an end. It is a long, intricate, intimate dance together and nothing matters more than your own sense of balance and your choice of partner.
~ Amy Bloom

Love is not altogether a delirium,
yet it has many points in common therewith.
~ Thomas Carlyle

Love in a Nutshell

Sanskrit has ninety-six words for love; ancient Persian, eighty; and Greek, four. But English has only one.[1] Even if our culture could understand the subtle nuances of ninety-six types of love, we would still have only one word, only four letters long to carry the weight of our relationships … our expectations … our marriages.

Love, therefore, is probably the most abused and misused word in the English language. Among its many definitions, love is described as

- a strong affection for another arising out of kinship or personal ties, such as the maternal *love* for a child;
- an attraction based on sexual desire, such as the affection and tenderness felt by lovers;
- an affection based on admiration, benevolence, or common interests, such as a *love* for an old friend;
- a warm attachment, enthusiasm, or devotion, as in a *love* of the sea;
- the object of attachment, devotion, or admiration, such as baseball was his first *love*;
- an unselfish loyal and benevolent concern for the good of another, as in the fatherly concern of God for humankind or a brotherly concern for others;

1

● an amorous episode, as in a *love* affair.[2]

As a culture, we use the word love to describe almost anything: sporting events, favorite foods, family pets, casual friends, and scores in a tennis match. At the same time, love is the word we use to describe our most intimate, passionate, and personal relationships.

Love—Greek Style

The Greeks have four words for love: *storge, eros, philia,* and *agape.* In the broadest sense, these words describe the four most elemental love relationships.

Storge is affectionate love. It's the warm and comfortable feeling of just being together. Like sea water and sand rubbing at a piece of glass until it is worn smooth with time, affection wears away our rough spots until we are comfortably creased and slightly tattered around the edges. Affection can be seen in the dog-eared pages of well-loved books and the worn-down soles of favorite shoes.

Almost anything or anyone can be the object of our affection. The only real criterion for storge love is that the item or person be familiar. That is why words like "old" and "always" are often associated with the people and possessions that we love affectionately.

Affection is the least-discriminating and most humble form of love. It can unite two things that have nothing in common other than their proximity to each other over a period of time. Picture for a moment the relationship between Belle and the Beast in *Beauty and the Beast*. Early in their relationship, while the Beast holds Belle prisoner in his castle, Belle is repulsed by him. But over time, she grows to see him as "sweet and almost kind" rather than "mean and ... coarse and unrefined." And just as their love blossoms into something more, so affection is often a foundation for other types of love. C. S. Lewis wrote:

> As gin is not only a drink in itself but also a base for many mixed drinks, so Affection, besides being a love itself, can enter into the other loves and colour them all through and become the very medium in which from day to day they operate.[3]

Affection is one of our basic human needs. Because we are raised in families, we expect affection from our parents and siblings. We are social creatures by nature, and we depend on the affection of our peers. In his hierarchy theory of motivation, Abraham Maslow ranks our need for affection and belonging right after our need for nourishment and security, but before our need for esteem or self-fulfillment. As human beings, we actually *need* other people—physically, emotionally, and intellectually—before we can really know anything about ourselves.

Eros, on the other end of the love spectrum, is the passionate, dizzying, and desirous emotion of being "in love." It is what the Greeks described as a divine state of madness. Sigmund Freud called it a transient psychosis. Jerome Travers interpreted it as being

> literally "out of one's mind," out of contact with reality, clinically crazed. And, that's why love is so delicious! For romantic love is a time of total fantasy, a euphoric condition which leaves us in a soporific delusion that the other person can make me feel wonderful and happy.[4]

It's no wonder then that we dream of living happily ever after. We all know the famous lyrics, "*Love is a many-splendored thing,*" "*Love lifts us up where we belong,*" and "*All you need is love.*"

My own perspective of falling in love is paradoxical: we fall in love with people who evoke in us the unresolved issues of our childhood and, at the same time, awake a dormant part of our personality.

Eros love thrives on deeply biological and unconscious factors that entice us into intimate couple relationships in order to resolve the emotional hurts of our parental relationships and complete unfinished business of the past.[5] It seems essential that the person we choose to love must exhibit, on an unconscious level, the traits of our opposite-sex parent.

At the same time, an eros love relationship awakens in us new feelings, imagination, and creativity. John Desteian says that "infatuation reanimates—freshens—the personality, and at the same time provides the energy to explore the mystery of the unique other person with whom one has fallen in love."[6]

When we fall in love, we are building reservoirs in which to store this powerful emotion that can be a source of love and affection in times when the relationship seems dry or distant.

Philia, the love of friendship, is the least natural type of love. It doesn't make us feel hot and bothered like eros or warm and fuzzy like storge. It doesn't occur naturally through time and proximity or through physical attraction. True friendship exists at the highest level of individuality between people who take pleasure in sharing their lives with each other.

It is absolutely possible to have a lover who is also a friend, but a love-affair is nothing like a friendship. Lovers are quite content to spend hours talking about love, but friendship must be about something other than friendship. What draws two people together as friends is a similarity that sets them apart from the group. Friendship isn't a love of instinct; it is love by choice. We love those who love us.

Agape, on the other hand, extends love from those who love us to those who don't. It is a love that is wholly disinterested in self and "desires what is simply best for the beloved."[7] It is the love that inspires someone to sacrifice his or her own life for that of another. It is agape that enables Sidney Carton to take the place of Charles Darnay at the guillotine in Charles Dickens's *A Tale of Two Cities* (1859).

Agape is love of divine principle of thought and action that modifies the character, governs the impulses, controls the passions, and glorifies the affections. It is love in its highest, truest form.

M. Scott Peck describes this love as "the will to extend one's self for the purpose of nurturing one's own or another's spiritual growth."[8] The act of extending ourselves requires effort because we can only extend our limits by exceeding them. When we love someone, our love becomes real through our actions—through the fact that, for someone we love, we are willing to walk an extra mile. This type of love is far from effortless.

By using the word "will," Peck clarifies the distinction between desire and action. Desire does not necessarily translate into action. Will, on the other hand, is desire of such intensity that it demands to be acted upon. Love is an act of will—both intention and action. Will also implies choice. We do not have to love. We choose to love.

And in many cases, those who choose to love also choose to marry.

The Motives for Marriage

In Western culture, many people view marriage as something magical that happens *to* them. In that divine state of madness, we experience an all-absorbing passion that brings us to the height of feeling and imagination. Time stands still, and in this great surge of energy and excitement, our thoughts continuously stray to the beloved person who makes our life complete.

Of course people marry, or form couple relationships, for a variety of other reasons as well: common interests; mutual support or companionship; anticipation of happiness and fulfillment; to have children; to fulfill their parents' expectations; to get away from their family; a fear of being single or alone; on the rebound; couldn't say no; social status; sex or pregnancy; etc. These reasons have been with us since the beginning of time.

From ancient times up until the 1950s, marriage was essentially an economic arrangement. Women married men who would support them; men married women with dowries. Women served men by fulfilling their sexual desires, bearing legal children, and caring for the home. Men provided food, shelter, and protection for their wives and children. These early roles and responsibilities set the stage for many of today's legal, religious, and social aspects of marriage.

The church first entered into marriage relationships in the Middle Ages, transforming the economic arrangement into a holy sacrament. Although marriage no longer required parental consent, it was a sacramental holy union that could not be dissolved, no matter how miserable either partner may have been.

During the Protestant Reformation, marriage lost its sacramental status but did not diminish in the eyes of the church. Although the new wedding vows published in England's 1522 *Book of Prayer* put more emphasis on help and comfort for both husband and wife, husbands still retained authority, even ownership, over their wives.

In early American history, the Puritans viewed marriage as a civil contract between two people that could be dissolved like any other contract. Although divorce in the new colony was rare, it occurred more frequently than in England and was usually initiated by women. Divorced women were encouraged to marry again to avoid the temptations of adultery and fornication.

Modern Western marriages, wherein love is the primary reason for selecting a partner, evolved during the period between the American Revolution and the 1830s. Social historians point to several reasons for this shift, including a general revolutionary spirit that released children from their parents' authority, a romantic backlash to the Age of Reason that focused on the emotions rather than the intellect, and the rapid movement toward industrialization that relocated young adults away from their parents' watchful eyes.

For the upper class, marriage ensured that women need not work outside the home. While the husband provided, the wife was responsible for obeying her husband, satisfying his needs, caring for the physical and moral needs of the children, and managing the household (or the servants who managed the household).

The early 1900s saw the rise of the Women's Movement that likened marriage to the bondage of slavery and westward expansion that inspired an increase in mail-order brides. In 1920, Margaret Sanger's advocacy for birth control gave men and women more power over the number of their offspring and enabled more women to move into public life.

World Wars I and II had a dramatic impact on marriage relationships by shaking up employment patterns. During World War II, women entered the workforce in unprecedented numbers, taking jobs that supported the war effort or that were vacated by men fighting overseas. For the first time in history, there were more married than single women in the workforce. This was partly due to the urgency of young couples to marry before the men left to fight. By 1944, there were 2.5 million more married women in the workforce than in 1940.[9] The increase in the number of working women led to the development of federally funded day-care centers. The income earned by women gave them more control over family financial decisions.

Following the war, women in the workforce led to increased marital tension. Women in some professions were accused of taking jobs away from deserving men, and husbands whose wives continued to work were viewed as poor providers. Women also found it difficult to give up their authority over the household when their husbands returned home. At the same time, men struggled with the physical, emotional, and psychological scars of war and with the process of readjusting to civilian life. In light of these pressures, many wartime marriages fell apart. By 1946, the divorce rate had risen to one in every four marriages.[10]

But on the surface, it was difficult to see the crumbling foundation. The 1950s, often depicted as a decade of domestic bliss, saw women re-embrace the role of wife and mother and saw men restored as the primary providers. Magazines began to publish articles about "making marriage work," encouraging women to devote their lives to pleasing their husbands in every way.

That was over fifty years ago, when men and women typically married someone from the same geographic region who shared a similar ethnicity, religion, and family background. Most women didn't have sex before marriage, or at least not until they had an engagement ring. Marriage usually ended a woman's education, and children typically ended any type of career. Relatively few people around the couple were divorced, and marriage was viewed as a lifetime commitment.

The 1960s saw a rebellion toward this way of life in the form of a sexual revolution where "free love" (and by that we really mean "sex") without commitment led to increased co-habitation. Women in many levels of society became active in political affairs and voiced their feminist independence by reentering the workforce. The same era saw more men take up household tasks. With the passage of *Roe v. Wade* in 1973, legalized abortion gave men and women even more power over the reproductive process, increasing the options for couples to delay parenthood while participating in sexual relationships.

Today, the roles of husband and wife are as vague as they have ever been. Marriage no longer guarantees financial security for women or domestic tranquility for men. Marriage isn't even a prerequisite for parenthood in an era where as many as 40 percent of American children are born outside of a marriage relationship. In terms of finances, careers, sex, and child rearing, the modern marriage has no set roles other than those ingrained in us by centuries of history and by our experiences with our own families. In describing the modern marriage, Marilyn Yalom writes:

> The old system of husbands providing and women raising children has broken down. Both people contribute to the family budget but women still do most of the domestic work. The old structure has broken down, but it hasn't been fully replaced by a new model—so everyone has to make up their own.[11]

As far as families are concerned, more changes have taken place in the last fifty years than have occurred in the last one hundred years. The divorce rate has skyrocketed to 50 percent, more women are working, more single parents are raising children alone, and psychologists are inundated with more family and marital problems than we dreamed possible. I've seen more cases involving sexual abuse, rape, and battered women in the past ten to fifteen years than I did in all of my previous years as a therapist combined. On the other hand, I am also seeing more and more couples who want to save their marriages and understand each other.

A Theory that Complements Technique

When I obtained my license as a marriage and family therapist in 1967, there were no theories or road maps for doing marital therapy. In fact, Gerald I. Manus said in 1966 that marital therapy was "a technique in search of a theory."[12] As I dealt with a growing number of troubled marriages into the 1970s, I realized that the marriage relationship is a developmental process that unfolds over time. Drawing on the contributions of clinical psychology and psychiatry, family systems therapy, family sociology, and social psychology to the growing body of marriage and family literature, I developed a model that maps the journey shared by couples across six unique marital stages: honeymoon, expectation, power struggle, seven-year-itch, reconciliation, and acceptance.

As they travel through these stages, husbands and wives not only lay the foundation for their couple relationship, but they also develop a clearer understanding of their identities as unique individuals—which makes marriage a little more complex than most people imagine.

I have used this marriage model with nearly 2,400 couples with an overwhelmingly positive response. Of those couples who have come through my office, an average of only one couple per year chooses divorce over restoring their relationship.

As you read through the following chapters, you may see yourself in one or more of these stages. The exciting thing about this realization is that you can use the tools provided in each chapter to tackle the developmental tasks necessary to transition into the next stage both as individuals and as a couple.

It is my desire that as you work through these tasks, you and your partner will (1) explore and develop your own identities; (2) further your understanding of individual, couple, and family dynamics; (3) increasingly value each other as unique individuals; and (4) lay a foundation for a relationship based on mutual love and respect for each person's individuality and a commitment to each other.

As you work toward reconciliation and acceptance, you will be able to assess your problem areas and resolve the unfinished business of the past that creates obstacles in the path toward an intimate and enduring relationship.

No Man Is an Island

This basic human longing to refind our core wholeness
is the essence of religion and poetry
and the essence of the ecstacies of perfect love.
~ Louise J. Kaplan
(*Oneness and Separateness*)

Becoming an Individual

In *Devotions Upon Emergent Occasions*, John Donne wrote, "No man is an island, entire of itself; every man is a piece of the continent, a part of the main." When it comes to relationships, this famous meditation is right on target. No one, man or woman, simply emerges from time and space without a connection to the past. For better or for worse, we are born into generations of history—and that's where life gets complicated because there are no perfect parents. Neither are there any perfect children.

And yet the family ties that bind (and sometimes gag) are the same threads that make up the fabric of who we are as individuals. Are you loyal, cautious, creative, thrifty, patient, or suspicious? Do you make your bed every day? Are you afraid of cats? Do you underestimate your abilities or over commit your time? These seem like silly questions, I know, but your answers are most likely rooted in some aspect of your past.

The qualities and quirks that we carry into adulthood are almost always nurtured in our childhood. That being the case, there are three specific elements of childhood that significantly impact your intimate relationships as an adult. I like to call these elements the "building blocks" of marriage. They include:

- Your separation-individuation process
- Your parents' model of marriage
- Your family's beliefs and behaviors

Psychoanalytic[1] developmental theorists believe that children's psychic[2] structures evolve from the process of separation-individuation (letting go) between parent and child. As adults, this process of drawing close and letting go repeats itself in our relationships with others. In a marriage, this process is the foundation of each person's identity. It is the "I" that each person brings into the relationship.

The development of the "we" in a couple relationship is influenced both consciously and unconsciously by the other two elements: the parents' models of marriage and the beliefs and behaviors of each person's family of origin. These two building blocks identify the needs and wants that each person brings into the couple relationship.

Standing alone, these three elements are neither new nor original. They are borrowed from the rich contributions of talented practitioners to the fields of clinical psychology and psychiatry, family systems therapy, family sociology, and social psychology. In the context of the journey that is marriage, however, they come together to provide the backbone of preconceived notions that each and every one of us carry into our intimate adult relationships.

Separation-Individuation: Let Me Go but Don't Let Go

The grand adventure of becoming an individual is the cornerstone of human development and begins with the relationship between mother and child. The unconscious needs, wants, expectations, and conflicts that linger from this intensely intimate bond subtly shape the very foundation of who we are as individuals.

Childhood

In the earliest days of life, an infant receives all of its food, warmth, comfort, and security from a blissful relationship with its mother. Nothing can entice the child to explore beyond these trusted boundaries. Actively involved fathers and trusted caregivers are often included in this intimate circle within a few weeks.

---

1   **Psychoanalysis** is a method of analyzing psychic phenomena and treating emotional disorders that involves treatment sessions during which the patient is encouraged to talk freely about personal experiences, and especially about early childhood and dreams.

2   **Psychic** comes from the Greek *psychikos*, meaning "of the soul," and therefore existing outside the sphere of physical science or knowledge.

By the age of six months, however, it's a whole new ballgame. The child's expanding curiosity about the world beyond the parents' protective arms compels him or her to taste, touch, and try everything—at first by putting things in his or her mouth and then by crawling, walking, and running away.

In the first three years of life, children progress through increasingly complex stages of physical, emotional, cognitive, motor, moral, and linguistic development. Besides learning how to walk, talk, feed themselves, and use the potty, children are also actively involved in forming their own identities. Is it any wonder then that children take such delight in the word "no"? As they explore the consequences of making independent choices, they begin to see themselves as separate beings and no longer as extensions of their parents.

During this separation-individuation process, children consistently test their boundaries as declarations of independence from mom and dad. "I do it!" is the childish battle cry of liberated toddlers everywhere. Through this process of trial and error, children begin to practice the unique qualities, characteristics, and abilities needed to function in the world around them. Later in adolescence and adulthood, these accomplishments and self-discovery experiences come together to form one's identity.

Therefore, the ways in which a child lets go of his or her parents and his or her success in developing a separate identity sets the stage for future relationships and personal growth. As poet and playwright Eleanor Farjoen once wrote, "The events of childhood do not pass, but repeat themselves like the seasons of the year"[1]

The Teen Years

The entire process of letting go repeats itself when toddlers become teenagers. In this period of increasing independence, teenagers often draw their sense of identity from their friendships rather than their parents. In fact, the driving force behind adolescent behavior is often to veer as far from the parental path as possible, even to the point of bodily injury or death, hence the hairstyles, the music, the movies, the clothes, the piercings, the broken curfews, and the hours spent on the phone. Even teens with healthy parental relationships push the envelope in defining their own identities—like the straight-A student-body president who gets a tattoo over spring break or the young man who circumvents his school's dress code by donning a tie constructed entirely out of duct tape.

In a successful teenage separation-individuation, the young person is able to successfully separate from the parents' identity while still being involved in the family.[2] Independence for young people doesn't necessarily mean isolation. It's a feeling of separation while remaining connected. It's like knowing that if they jump off the bridge, the bungee cord will be there to pull them back to safety.

Young Adulthood

How a person eventually leaves his or her family and home represents another separation-individuation experience. Whenever I encounter clients struggling with separation issues, I ask them to explore the thoughts, feelings, and events that surrounded their departures from their families of origin. Did they leave home with their families' blessings and encouragement to pursue their own dreams? Did they graduate from high school and move out the next day? Did they run away? What happened next?

Leaving home is a very critical transition period because the way that we handle leaving the family relationship is the way that we tend to deal with all separation issues thereafter. Those who view it as an escape are likely to repeat that behavior in future difficult relationships.

If it was a traumatic experience, you will always feel wounded. It's as if all of your roots have been ripped from the ground, leaving you parched, withered, and alone. People who experience traumatic transitions continue to grieve until they heal the past hurts and take root in new relationships.

Marriage

Within the context of an enduring adult relationship, there is yet another opportunity to expand, refine, and consolidate our identities by exploring who we are as men and women, husbands and wives, and mothers and fathers. At this point, not only are we developing identities as individuals, but we are also in the process of developing an identity as a couple. This process may also be continuous with parenthood. One process doesn't always stop and wait for the other!

The separation-individuation process is one of the essential building blocks in creating an intimate and enduring relationship. It establishes the boundaries that will permit emotional intimacy, even merging, without a fear of losing yourself.

When people do not fully and successfully develop their own identities in childhood or adolescence, this unfinished business from the past—this lack of self—eventually erodes the marriage relationship. As M. Grotjahn writes, "Marriage partners continue from approximately the point at which respective parents left off … people bring into the marriage their past in order to repeat it; it is their duty and fate to try and master it."[3] This is a significant task. Until both you and your partner resolve your unfinished business with your parents, neither of you will be able to achieve a sense of wholeness and belonging in your marriage.

When marriages dissolve through death or divorce, we once again have an opportunity for continued evolution of the identity. If we choose to remarry, the process starts all over again. In fact, whenever we go through a major transition in life, we are confronted with the potential for change. And in the end, every aspect of humanity is reflected in the balance between independence and intimacy. As Louise Kaplan describes it:

> [E]ach time we enlarge the boundaries of our self, we re-experience the temporary limbo of suddenly not knowing who we were or who we might become. Yet as adults we continue to push out from our confining boundaries. We cut ourselves loose. We declare ourselves free of the safety of home base and inevitably we return. The cycle of breaking free and returning to base is one that we are engaged in as long as we are truly alive.[4]

The separation-individuation process is the foundation of the "I" in marriage. Now let's examine the evolution of the "we" in a relationship.

The Apple Doesn't Fall Far from the Tree

Family faces are magic mirrors.
Looking at people who belong to us,
we see the past, present, and future.
~ Gail Lumet Buckley

Reflecting Your Parents' Relationship

In my years as a marriage and family therapist, I've come to believe George Santayana when he wrote, "Those who do not study history are doomed to repeat it." I see this happening over and over again in families and relationships. I see couples taking on roles and repeating patterns handed down through the generations like treasured heirlooms.

When it comes to relationships, the apple doesn't fall very far from the tree at all. What we learn from our parents' marriage (or possibly marriages) is the second building block in constructing our own intimate adult relationships.

It's important to remember that not all of the beliefs and behaviors that we carry from generation to generation are inherently bad or wrong. After all, your partner grew up in a family and still managed to develop enough desirable traits to merit your undying love and affection, and so his or her parents must have done something right. But there are no perfect families, and it's likely that you both brought some baggage into your relationship. It's even more likely that you and your parents have matching sets of bags. In her guide to new brides, Marg Stark writes:

> The morning after her wedding … the bride wakes up with thirteen people in her honeymoon bed—her husband, her parents, her grandparents, his parents, and his grandparents. As unsavory a mental picture as this is, it's true that we all get hand-me-downs from our families. It is not just gender roles—dad takes out the garbage, mom does everything else—that are encoded in us, but many underlying

14

messages of marriage, including how we argue and how much happiness we expect to find in our relationships.[1]

Although our parents' marriage patterns can pop up anywhere in a new adult relationship, they are most likely to appear in highly emotional or stressful situations, both positive and negative. Think money, sex, power, work, in-laws, and division of household chores, and you're on the right track. Ask almost any married couple to list their "big issues," and their answers will likely boil down to one of these areas.

So why are these buttons so easy to push? Why do arguments about these issues end in screaming matches and slamming doors? At the core of our being, we are fiercely loyal to our families. This loyalty develops at a very young age, as we see from the experiences of a boy named Charlie.

> *Eight-year-old Charlie had two younger sisters. When his mother went into the hospital to deliver her fourth child, Charlie desperately wanted a brother. What he got was another sister. Charlie was furious. He refused to go to the hospital to visit his mother or the new baby. When they came home from the hospital, he refused to acknowledge the baby girl's existence. And then one day, one of his friends looked at his baby sister and said, "That's the ugliest baby I've ever seen." Charlie brushed it off and went on playing. But his mother said that later that evening she found him leaning over the baby's cradle, stroking her head and saying, "I am your big brother and I will protect you. I am never going to let anyone ever be mean to you again."*

Like Charlie, you may not always like your family, but they're yours. When someone attacks your family's way of life (especially when that someone is a marriage partner whose parents did everything differently), sparks are going to fly.

In the latter half of this book, we'll be working through the six stages of modern marriage. Stages one through five address the idea of redefining your relationship and expanding your boundaries to find the roles and responsibilities that work best for you and your partner in the present. But the very fact that there is a need for redefinition implies that some assumptions, expectations, roles, and responsibilities already exist. In almost every case, the preexisting template is a reflection of your parents' relationship. Let's take a look at a few of the hot-button issues.

Money

Money itself is not the cause of our problems. There are really only three things that we can do with money: earn it, save it, or spend it. What complicates money matters are our emotional attachments to each of these activities. Inevitably, a saver will marry a spender, and each adds his or her own attitude to the mix. What the saver sees as responsible fiscal behavior, the spender views as hoarding. What the spender sees as harmless fun, the saver considers wasteful. When you face emotionally charged money arguments, ask yourselves the following questions:

1. Who was the primary bread winner in your family?

    _____

    _____

2. Did both of your parents work to support the family?

    _____

    _____

3. Who managed the family money?

    _____

    _____

4. Did your family operate within a budget?

    _____

    _____

5. Did your parents have separate or joint checking accounts?

    _____

    _____

6. Who was a saver and who was a spender?

_____

_____

7. What was the general attitude about money in your family? (For example, was money for saving, for spending, for giving, or for having fun?)

_____

_____

Do you see any patterns or beliefs about money repeating in your relationship? Do they work for you? If not, identify the source of the stress, and separate it from the current situation.

Problem Patterns: Money	
Past	Anna's father earned all of the family money, and her mother always had to ask for money anytime she wanted to buy something for herself, the home, or the children.
Present	Anna views having her own money as a sign of freedom and independence. Eric (Anna's husband) wants to combine their money into one checking account, and Anna is afraid of ending up in the same situation as her mother.
Result	Anna and Eric argue about money all of the time. Eric thinks Anna doesn't trust him with money. Anna is worried that Eric will control her if she doesn't have her own resources.
Resolution	Anna and Eric developed a family budget that included monthly amounts of money for different needs (food, mortgage, clothes, gasoline, etc.). Once Anna could see that their needs would be met and that she had the freedom to spend within the budget without asking Eric for money, she was much more comfortable about combining their resources into a single checking account.

Affection and Sexuality

Everybody expresses his or her sexuality differently. Some people are very comfortable in their own skin and relish the idea of open displays of physical affection. Others are more private or reserved. Our parents' love lives will impact our own. American clergyman Theodore Hesburgh once said, "The most important thing a father can do for his children is to love their mother."

People who grow up in openly loving households are more secure about pursuing those same types of relationships as adults. Children of divorce or abuse have a much harder time forming romantic, affectionate, or trusting bonds in adult relationships. On a smaller scale, openness and comfort levels about physical affection and sex education are also carried from generation to generation (even if there is a pendulum effect in which the following generation carries out the exact opposite behavior of the preceding generation). When you and your partner are at odds over affection or intimacy, ask yourselves the following questions:

1. How did your parents express love and affection?

    _____

    _____

2. How did you know that they loved each other?

    _____

    _____

3. How did your parents express love and affection toward their children?

    _____

    _____

4. Were your parents physically affectionate with you in a positive way (appropriate hugging, kissing, etc.)?

    _____

    _____

5. Did your parents teach you about sex, or did you obtain that knowledge from another source?

_____

_____

6. What messages about body image (weight, beauty, hygiene, etc.) did you see expressed in your family?

_____

_____

If the answers to any of these questions reveal the possibility of abuse or inappropriate conduct, I would encourage you to explore those issues with a professional therapist. Otherwise, take some time to think about the affectionate, physical, and sexual roles you and your partner currently carry out. Do you like a lot of affection? When and where are you comfortable expressing and receiving affection? Do you enjoy a lot of physical contact or do you need more personal space? Are you confident expressing your sexuality or do you need some encouragement? Do you prefer to be the initiator or the recipient in a sexual relationship? After you've taken some time to reflect, decide whether or not these roles work for your relationship.

Problem Patterns: Affection and Sexuality	
Past	Jared's parents were very affectionate with each other. When his father arrived home from work, he would find Jared's mother making dinner and kiss her in the kitchen in front of the children.
Present	When Jared arrives in the evening, his wife Elizabeth is frustrated with his affectionate behavior. She shrugs off his kisses and asks him to leave her alone.
Result	Jared and Elizabeth have a fairly strained sexual relationship. Elizabeth often feels smothered, and Jared feels rejected.

Resolution	Thinking back on her parents' relationship, Elizabeth zeroed in on how much her father appreciated her mother's cooking. To Elizabeth, being a loving wife meant preparing great meals for Jared. His amorous interruptions drove her crazy because she felt like he didn't appreciate the effort that she was putting into dinner. When Jared explained that affection was more important than the meals, Elizabeth was able to relax when he wanted to be near her in the kitchen. When Jared understood Elizabeth's desire to cook for him, he agreed to give her some space if they could agree to be affectionate at another time in the evening.

As you work through issues of affection, intimacy, and sexuality, keep in mind that just because you and your partner don't express your love in the same way, it doesn't mean that you don't love each other. In *The Five Love Languages*, Dr. Gary Chapman outlines five different ways through which people express and receive love: acts of service, quality time, words of affirmation, gifts, and physical touch.[2] In the scenario above, Elizabeth expressed her love through acts of service while Jared expressed his through physical touch. The way that you give love is often the way that you want to receive it as well. To develop a more intimate relationship, spend some time learning about your partner's "love language."

In the case of couples who struggle with physical contact and personal space, I like to use an exercise in which each partner stands against the wall on opposite sides of a room. I ask one partner to walk toward the other (who remains against the wall). The walking partner advances until the stationary partner feels uncomfortable with the amount of space between them and asks him or her to stop. This will let both partners visually see the personal boundaries of the stationary partner. Repeat the exercise and reverse roles to determine the space needs of the other person. When both people can experience each other's comfort levels, they have a starting point for negotiating future physical contact.

Power

In *As You Like It*, William Shakespeare wrote, "All the world is a stage, and all the men and women merely players. They have their exits and entrances; each man in his time plays many parts."[3] Relationships are also stages. But in this case, men and women are players struggling for power. In any love relationship, after the initial passionate fury of romance fades, one or both people shed their inhibitions and ask themselves: *Can I really be myself in this relationship? Will my partner still love me if I express how I really feel? What if I want to do something my way? What if I disagree? Will I be accepted?* They begin to test the waters, to take a stand, to act out different roles.

The battle to resolve a power struggle can take on a variety of forms: silence, withdrawal, ambivalence, distrust, anger, blame, an emotional tug-of-war, and even verbal or physical abuse. In most cases, the roles we choose are those modeled by one or both of our parents. If you and your partner are engaged in a power struggle, you could jump straight to chapter nine, or you could take a few moments to ask yourselves the following questions:

1. Did your parents engage in an ongoing power struggle?

    _____

    _____

2. If so, what was the heart of the issue (money, sex, careers, time, etc.)?

    _____

    _____

3. Who was the more dominant figure in your parents' relationship?

    _____

    _____

4. Who was the more passive figure?

    _____

    _____

5. How did your parents resolve their differences?

    _____

    _____

6. Were your parents emotionally responsive to each other's needs?

_____

_____

Many people believe that if they simply leave a power-struggle relationship, their problems will go away. Although separation or divorce might provide temporary relief from the cycle of blame and accusation, the old saying "wherever you go, there you are" certainly applies. If you don't take the time to deal with *your* contribution to the struggle, the same issues will be waiting for you in each subsequent relationship.

Problem Patterns: Power	
Past	Lena grew up in a father-dominated household. She and her sisters had little influence over any aspect of their lives, including who they could marry and whether or not they could go to university.
Present	Mark and Lena just bought their first house and are locked in a power struggle over how to redecorate it. Mark inherited a lot of family heirlooms and wants to use them in the décor. Lena wants to buy all new furniture.
Result	Both Mark and Lena are trying to work on the project when the other isn't around. While Mark was out of town, Lena took out a $5,000 loan to hire a painter and install new carpet. To retaliate, Mark moved all of his furniture out of storage and into their house.
Resolution	In looking back over their parents' relationships, Lena was able to determine that her intense need to control this situation came from the lack of control that she saw in her mother's life and had experienced in her own childhood. She didn't understand Mark's desire to honor his family by preserving their heirlooms. She viewed his actions as his desire to control their home the way that her father had. As a compromise, Lena agreed to use Mark's family's furniture in some of the rooms if they could redecorate their bed and bathroom

	with new items. When Mark realized the full extent of Lena's feelings, he included her in more of the decision making process.

The balance of power within a relationship is at the root of almost every disagreement. When you find yourself locked in a repetitive, emotional, or intense power struggle with your partner, look to the patterns of the past to see if you're repeating them in the present.

Work

Work is a tricky issue because its roots are tightly wound around money and power, particularly for women. In an era where marriage no longer guarantees financial security for either partner, the questions of who will work, when, and for how long are ones that every couple needs to answer. People work either because they want to (they find fulfillment and joy in their chosen careers) or because they have to (in order to provide for their families), and the roles in each relationship are different.

The issue of work is particularly significant in this day and age where traditional gender roles—dad works and mom stays home—are no longer the norm. Although more men are taking on household and parenting roles, and more women are working outside of the home, the undercurrent of our society still clings to a *Leave it to Beaver* mindset. We're playing new roles—Mr. Mom and Mrs. CEO—with very few ground rules. If you or your partner struggle with this balance, ask yourselves the following questions:

1. Did both of your parents work, or only one or the other?

   _____

   _____

2. What was your father's attitude about work?

   _____

   _____

3. What was his opinion of working women?

_____

_____

4. Did your mother work?

_____

_____

5. Did she work because she wanted to or because she needed to?

_____

_____

6. Was either of your parents a workaholic?

_____

_____

7. Was either of your parents unemployed for long periods of your childhood?

_____

_____

Like Jack and Patty in the following vignette, you may have lingering past concerns that are slowly eroding your present relationship.

Problem Patterns: Work	
Past	Jack's father was often unemployed when he was growing up. As a result, his mother had to take on part-time jobs to make ends meet, leaving her with little time to care for Jack and his two brothers.

Present	Jack is currently out of work. His wife Patty worked as a registered nurse before they were married, but Jack refuses to let her work while he is unemployed.
Result	The family is struggling financially, and Patty feels like Jack doesn't value the work that went into earning her degree. Jack is embarrassed that he cannot provide for his family and is taking his anger and frustration out on Patty and their children.
Resolution	Jack needed to work through his feelings toward his father. He resented the way that his dad's irresponsibility had forced his mom to work when she didn't really want to. Jack didn't want to do the same to Patty, but by refusing to let her work, he left her feeling useless. They ultimately agreed that Patty would go back to nursing three days a week, and Jack would care for the children. On the other two days, he would be free to look for work or go to job interviews. It took a lot of humility for Jack to agree to the plan, but when Patty felt like she was contributing and they were able to pay their bills, they felt like a team again.

Work is one area where there truly is no one-size-fits-all solution. Not only must you decide what's right for your relationship, but you must also manage the consequences of your decision. We live in a schizophrenic society in which both working mothers and stay-at-home mothers take heat for their choices. Husbands who work long hours so that their wives can stay home are accused of being uninvolved parents. But those who arrange their work schedules around their families are criticized for their lack of ambition on the job. I say this to remind you that there is no magic solution. You and your partner truly need to make this decision together and to reevaluate your positions as your lives change.

In-Laws

In-law relationships are multigenerational by design, but they often reach back an additional generation or two. As Marg Stark so aptly noted earlier, when we marry someone, we marry that person's parents and grandparents as well. And just as you have expectations about how you'll be treated in the marriage relationship, they also have expectations about how you'll treat their adult child or grandchild—and them. Tension builds when you (or your partner) act outside of those expectations.

Our earliest model of in-law relationships is built on how our parents interact with our grandparents. If you and your partner are struggling with in-law relationships—particularly surrounding the issues of time (who gets more of it) and money (who's still running home to the First National Bank of Dad for a loan)—ask yourselves the following questions:

1. How did your parents interact with their in-laws?

    _____

    _____

2. Did they have a loving relationship or was there tension?

    _____

    _____

3. If there was tension, what was at the heart of the issue?

    _____

    _____

4. Were their attitudes obvious to you as child?

    _____

    _____

5. How did your parents eventually resolve these issues?

    _____

    _____

6. How do they handle them now?

    _____

As Lauren discovers in the following vignette, memories of old experiences can hinder growth in new relationships.

Problem Patterns: In-Laws	
Past	Jeff's parents love to visit their children's families and often plan extended vacations around visits, announcing to the couples when they will arrive and depart and how they want to spend their time while they're in town. They never ask if it is a good time to visit or if the length of time works with Jeff and Amy's schedule.
Present	Jeff and Amy's daughter Lauren is now married with in-laws of her own. One weekend, Lauren's mother-in-law sent an e-mail to the family saying that she would be driving through town and planned to stay with Lauren and Chad. Lauren was furious with Chad for letting his mother announce her arrival rather than asking if it was okay to visit.
Result	Chad was upset with Lauren for assuming that his mother wanted to control their family. Lauren was upset because she didn't want to develop the type of relationship with her mother-in-law that she saw her mother experience. She wanted it dealt with immediately.
Resolution	After she was able to separate herself from the emotions of her mother's situation, Lauren was able to explain her concerns to Chad. Chad then called his mom and told her that they'd be happy to have her spend the night but would appreciate being asked in the future. He also told his mom (with Lauren's permission) about the relationship between Lauren's mom and paternal grandmother to explain why they felt the need to lay the ground rules. His mother was upset by the request at first, but she eventually accepted the idea and has since spent many happy weekends with the couple.

If you did not establish healthy and flexible boundaries with your in-laws early in your relationship, it's never too late to start. But you will only be successful in creating change in the relationship if you and your partner are working as a team.

Household Chores

And we're right back to power (who has it) and work (who does it). It's amazing how these things are all connected, and it's tough to talk about household chores without jumping up onto the gender-equality soapbox. The bottom line is that women still handle the bulk of household responsibilities, whether they work outside the home or not.

In 1989, Arlie Hochschild addressed this issue in her book *The Second Shift*. Using estimates from the 1960s and 1970s, she measured the time women spent doing a paid job as well as housework and childcare and discovered that women work roughly fifteen hours longer than men each week. That adds up to an extra month and twenty-four days each year, or a year of twenty-four-hour days every twelve years.[4]

If you and your partner do not agree on the balance of labor on the home front, the lingering resentment and frustration felt by one or both of you will color other aspects of your relationship, including your sex life.

If you and your partner are struggling with your beliefs and behaviors over the division of household chores, ask yourselves the following questions:

1. How did your parents divide household responsibilities?

    _____

    _____

2. Did they work together or use a divide-and-conquer approach?

    _____

    _____

3. What was your father's attitude toward household chores?

    _____

    _____

4. What about your mother's?

_____

_____

5. What chores were you responsible for as a child?

_____

_____

6. What chores do you love to do, and what do you despise doing?

_____

_____

Do you see any patterns or beliefs about who does what around the house repeating in your relationship? Do they work for you? If not, identify the source of the stress, and separate it from the current situation. Then work with your partner to find a positive solution.

Problem Patterns: Household Chores	
Past	Robin has never mowed a lawn in her life. As a child, yard work was primarily the responsibility of her father or brothers. Although she had her own list of chores, they were primarily relegated to indoor work.
Present	Robin and Dan recently bought their first house after five years in an apartment, and the amount of work needed to keep their home running has increased significantly. They initially decided to split the chores into indoor and outdoor, with Dan taking the outside and Robin taking the inside chores.

Result	Robin resents the fact that Dan can accomplish most of his chores on Saturday while her chores spread throughout the whole week. When she asks Dan for help, he argues that they made a deal and that he's keeping up his part. Dan also asks Robin to help with the outside jobs, which drives her crazy because she's already doing more.
Resolution	Robin and Dan both sat down and made a list of all of the things that they had taken responsibility for, how often those tasks had to be accomplished, and how long they took to accomplish. They also looked over the list and tried to identify which tasks they had been taught as children and which ones they saw their respective parents do. After looking at the list, Dan realized that Robin really was doing more and agreed to take on several of the things from her list. But he also expressed feelings of loneliness because they spent most of their weekends accomplishing separate tasks. When he explained that he wanted Robin's help outside so that he could spend more time with her, she realized that his requests were motivated by love and not by selfishness. Now they revisit their lists every few months to make sure that they are both getting things done and have time left over to do the things they enjoy.

From the day that women entered the paid workforce, household chores have been a point of stress or contention. In a book focused on the journey of modern marriage, it's almost discouraging to see ourselves living in the biography of previous generations. We're afraid to fall into the ruts that we saw our parents carve out, but we're also afraid to move forward into the unknown. But that is just what marriage is—a journey into the unknown. And that's what gives marriage so much potential. You and your partner do not have to embrace the road paved by previous generations. You can take a detour and chart your own course, but be aware that there may be potholes along the way.

Postcards from the Edge

When I work with individuals trapped in reflections of their parents' relationships, I encourage them to write, but not send, letters to their parents. These letters can take on several different tones. The writer might confront a parent, ask how they handled a particular situation in their own relationship, or question why they behaved in a certain way.

By putting words on paper but not sending the letters, many adults are able to work through their wounds without engaging in serious or damaging emotional contact. However, the process of writing the letters often gives them the courage to confront the parents who hurt them in person. Many of my clients go back to their families to heal old wounds after they are married. When they do go home, I encourage them to:

- Be observers. Instead of jumping into the family dynamic as soon as you walk through the door, sit back and watch. Remove yourself from the firing line, and give yourself some space to observe what's really happening.

- Listen to the script. Most families repeat the same arguments and scenarios over and over again. What ideas and beliefs are being repeated, and how have you bought into them?

- Look for their part. By observing the action and listening to the script, are you able to see the part that you usually play in each scene? Is that who you want to be?

After working through their own feelings about the situation, my clients are then able to address their parents and their partners with a new perspective. These same skills will also come in handy as you explore the beliefs and behaviors that you learned from your family of origin.

Assumptions Are Deadly!

Family love is messy, clinging, and of an annoying
and repetitive pattern like bad wallpaper.
~ Friedrich Nietzsche

Beliefs and Behaviors

The third building block of marriage comes from the beliefs and behaviors learned in our families of origin. The messages that we absorb as children have a nifty habit of reappearing in our adult relationships. They sneak into the workplace, our marriages, our parenting, and even our friendships. It's incredibly natural to see our families' beliefs and behaviors reflected in other relationships because they are so familiar and comfortable to us, even if they aren't working. Ninety-nine percent of my clients end up in therapy because they are trying to function in new relationships (a marriage, as a parent, etc.) by using old beliefs and behaviors.

All couples enter marriage with at least one set of structures and processes from each family of origin. As the couple starts to create their new relationship together, they begin to recreate these familiar structures and processes because each person has his or her own concept or definition of relationship and family.

> **Structures:** the family's roles, rules, communication patterns, and boundaries.
>
> **Processes:** how each family member functions in relation to one another.

How did your family members express love and affection? How did they solve problems and resolve conflict? How did they spend money? How did they have fun together? All of these family experiences will influence how you deal with these same issues in your adult relationships.

Even for people who vow to do everything differently when they have families of their own, their family-of-origin beliefs and behaviors are still the starting point for every relationship. They are the mark against which we compare all other systems of behavior. They are imprinted on our memories because they are the only experiences that we know.

Carrying our old structures and processes into other relationships isn't always a negative experience, but as Patricia Farrell points out, "it does always have a tremendous impact on how you feel about yourself and how you relate to others."[1]

Each person in a family plays several roles. A woman is not only a woman but also a daughter and perhaps a sister. When she marries, she becomes a wife; when children arrive, she becomes a mother. A man may be a son, a brother, and later a husband and father. Within our families, we interact with each other in all of these different roles.

In addition to these positions in the family, we also take on roles and responsibilities that fulfill the needs and expectations of ourselves and others. For example, a child may become a caretaker for his or her younger siblings at an early age in response to a mother's need for help. Children are very perceptive and will often sacrifice their own childish wants and desires to fulfill their parents' needs.

In most circumstances, our primary response to an emotional event is to relieve stress, and so we migrate toward the roles that balance out stressful situations. It's a bit of a juggling act with different family members swirling around the family circle. When one child takes on the role of "the responsible one," another child will inevitably embrace the balancing "irresponsible" role. The "lazy" child mirrors the "smart" child. The "clown" seeks to draw attention away from the "steady and serious" child. Each family produces the roles necessary for its own survival, and to an extent this is normal and healthy.

The danger arises when these rules and roles become so rigid and inflexible that they trap people in stereotypical situations, incapable of any growth or change that might result in a more fulfilling or satisfying relationship.

Fortunately, if anyone does get stuck in a role that doesn't work for them (and sometimes we've reached our thirties, forties, or beyond before we realize that change is necessary), they can change. The beliefs and behaviors that we learn as children can always be unlearned. By dealing with unresolved issues from the past, we can experience more satisfying, gratifying, and intimate relationships.

The Family Genogram

I love the veracity of Leo Tolstoy's opening line of *Anna Karenina*: "All happy families are like one another; each unhappy family is unhappy in its own way."[2] Although this classic tale is a work of fiction, the same passion, heartbreak, and destruction of those poignant first words still echo in today's broken families.

Getting to the root of unhappiness is the first step toward restoring your relationship, and it often requires a trip down memory lane.

I like to use genograms early in therapy sessions to help my clients identify and understand how their families of origin impact their present relationships. A genogram (pronounced *jen*-uh-gram) is a convenient way to map out family relationships. First developed and used in clinical settings by Monica McGoldrick and Randy Gerson, genograms are a visual representation of the family tree that depict how different people are biologically, legally, and emotionally related over at least three generations.[3]

Most genograms include basic objective information about the number of families, the number of children in each family, birth order, and deaths. More detailed depictions might also include demographics, the strength of ties between individuals, patterns of illness or disorders (alcoholism, depression, diseases, etc.), types and dates of significant family events (marriage, birth, death, divorce, adoption, etc.), and significant life stresses for different family members.

A genogram can also be a valuable tool for disclosing triangular relationships, assumptions about roles (especially in marriage), unhealed wounds from the separation-individuation process, and family attitudes toward relationships, differentness, and communication.

I like to use genograms as frameworks for exploring current issues and concerns because they allow clients to trace multigenerational family patterns and to avoid blaming their partner or their parents for negative situations.

Again, I must emphasize that my goal in sharing this information is not to solve your problems by dumping your present conflicts on your parents or your past. You have to take responsibility for your life in the present. However, in most cases, present-day hang-ups are tied to unfinished business from the past.

Creating a genogram involves three levels of information: (1) outlining the family structure, (2) filling in family information, and (3) defining family relationships.

Outlining Family Structures

As with many things, different groups of people have different symbols and ways of depicting families. Don't get too hung up on the details; you can always adapt the symbols to your own style if needed. The important thing is that *you* are able to understand your genogram when it is completed. The following symbols will give you a good place to start.

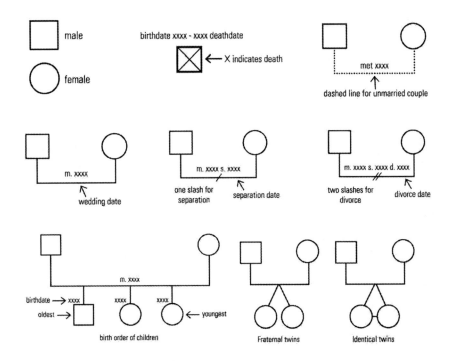

Below is a sample genogram for a woman named Anne.

Anne's Genogram

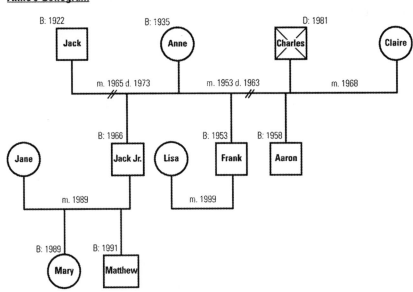

Using the symbols outlined above, what do you know about Anne based on her genogram?

She has been twice married and twice divorced.
Her first husband went on to remarry before his death.
Her second husband is still living.
She has three sons: two fathered by Charles and one by Jack.
In both of her marriages, a child was born within the first year of marriage.
Two of her sons are now married.
One of her sons has two children.

This basic factual information forms the basis of the genogram.

Filling in Family Information

After completing the basic family structure, it's time to add information about each individual including:

- Demographics (ages, dates of birth and death, locations, education levels, and jobs)
- Functions (objective data about medical, emotional, and behavioral issues)
- Critical family events (important transitions, relationships, losses, and successes)

Here is an example of Anne's genogram with some family information filled in.

Anne's Genogram

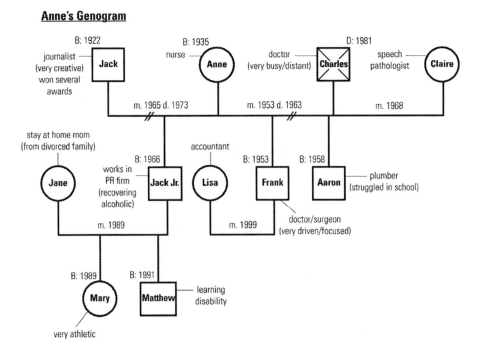

Defining Family Relationships

In this stage, different types of lines (squiggly, zigzag, dotted, etc.) are used to depict various types of relationships between family members. Are people very close or distant, conflicted, estranged, or loving? Sometimes these relationship patterns are so complex that they must be depicted on a separate genogram.

This is what Anne's family relationships look like in a genogram.

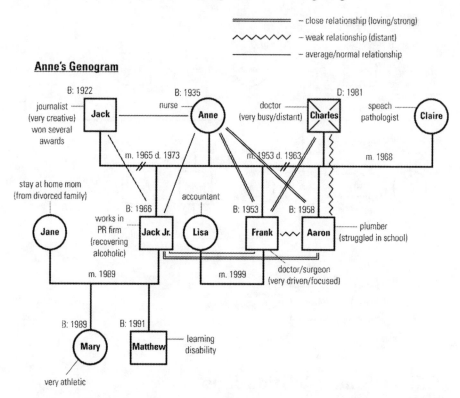

Equipped with all of this information, you can now examine a conflict in your current relationship within the context of your family beliefs and behaviors. A genogram can shed light on the familial, social, and historical perspectives of most issues. As we can see from the experiences of Lisa and David below, in many cases, the emotions underlying the present conflict have nothing to do with the marriage at all.

> *Three years into his marriage to Lisa, David began to withdraw from the relationship. Lisa wondered if she wasn't good enough or smart enough for David, if perhaps he was bored with her or regretting the relationship. This chipped away at her self-esteem until she asked David to go with her to marriage counseling. By tracing back through his family genogram, David realized that his retreat from Lisa was the result of unresolved grief over the loss of his father and sister, who died in a car accident when he was ten years old.*

In another case, where a husband was unwilling to forgive his wife for having an affair, his genogram revealed that he discovered his mother's affair when he was only six years old. Through couples therapy, he was able to understand that his unresolved anger, pain, and confusion about his mother's actions were restricting his ability to work through his wife's infidelity. Once he worked through his issues with his mother, he was also able to forgive his wife.

Often, when people can physically see in black and white how their partners are influenced by the relationships, rules, and roles at work in their families of origin, they no longer have a basis for blaming or attacking each other. The reality depicted in the genogram can move the couple into a more objective position from which to tackle their issues and concerns.

Recognizing and acknowledging family beliefs and behaviors—not to shift the blame but to understand their seductive pull—puts you in an ideal position to change how you think, act, and feel.

Moving On

Farrell describes family relationships as a dance in which each person has his or her own particular steps "according to some pattern that seemed long established and somehow safe."[4] Perhaps it's time to learn some new steps, to change the patterns of behavior from the past, to start a new song for the generations to follow. It sounds difficult, but it's not impossible.

Separate the Past from the Present

When an event in the present floods you with emotion, those emotions fade as soon as you deal with or acknowledge the event at hand. When an emotional response occurs and re-occurs in a patterned, predictable manner as if frozen in time, it is most likely rooted in the past. In these situations, take a step back and ask yourself the following questions: *When have I felt this way before? What was happening at the time? Who was involved?* If, as a child, Sunday was always a boring day for your family or if holidays always ended with Mom and Dad arguing in the front seat of the car, you may find yourself dreading Sundays or holidays with your partner.

When we fail to separate the past from the present, we end up in an emotional rut like Sam and Adrienne.

> *Sam used to complain that his wife Adrienne would "fly off the handle" and become furious at what appeared to be insignificant issues. She would become so angry that it actually took several hours for her to cool*

down after the arguments. When I explored this emotional response with Adrienne, she complained of feeling used and mistreated when Sam left his clothes on the bathroom floor rather than placing them in the laundry basket where they belonged. When I asked her who else made her feel used and mistreated, she looked away and whispered, "My father."

Adrienne's response had very little to do with Sam's actual behavior, although it did bother her. Her real issue was her relationship with her father and it was impacting her attitude toward Sam. This type of projection (in which we see our family of origin's unacceptable beliefs and behaviors in our partner) is one of the quickest ways to destroy a marriage relationship. So take the time to separate the realities of the current situation from your emotional ties to the past.

Retrain your Brain

When you understand the motivations behind your beliefs and behaviors, they become easier to change because you are able to tackle the past and the present as two separate events. When you find yourself reenacting the same emotionally charged situations over and over again, make two lists. On the first, list the events and feelings that the current problem drags up from the past. On the second, list the events and feelings related to the current problem. If Adrienne worked through this exercise, her lists might look something like this:

Angry w/Dad	Angry w/Sam
• My dad treated my mom really badly. • He didn't appreciate her or help with household chores. • He expected me to help my mom even though he didn't. • He didn't encourage me or praise me for my accomplishments. • This makes me feel unloved, unappreciated, and used. Remember that Sam is not my dad. Sam is not trying to hurt me. I am letting my emotions from my dad influence my attitude toward Sam!	• When Sam leaves his clothes on the floor it makes me angry. • I feel that he is being lazy and that he doesn't appreciate all of the work that I do around the house. • I feel that there is an expectation that I will always pick up after him and that he doesn't have to take any responsibility. • This makes me feel used and unappreciated.

	Solutions: • Explain feelings to Sam (tell him *why* I'm upset, not just that I *am* upset). • Ask Sam why he leaves clothes on the floor. Is *he* repeating a pattern? This is something that we can change together. • Ask Sam if there is a better place for the laundry basket, a place where he would be more likely to use it. • Come up with a consequence if he keeps doing it (maybe only washing clothes in the hamper, not the ones on the floor).

It takes a conscious effort to replace old patterns with new ones. It won't happen overnight, but if both you and your partner are willing to work toward change, it will happen. If you put all of these techniques into practice, and you're still replaying the same predictable problems three to six months down the road, it's time to seek outside help.

Give Yourself Room to Grow

The process of separating a present problem from an original wound takes time and patience from both partners. Give each other room to heal. Couples who work through their issues in an open and honest way strengthen their trust and open up their personal boundaries to find deeper intimacy. There is no end to the discoveries that two people can make together when they transcend the boundaries initiated for survival's sake by previous generations.

Mapping a Marriage

When love and skill work together, expect a masterpiece.
~ John Ruskin

Our Last Best Chance to Grow Up

Marriage is a dynamic and complex process. Comedian Paul Reiser describes it this way:

> Theoretically, marriage is all about Two people becoming as One. But in the real world—and let's be really clear about this—you ain't One. You're Two. And there's only so much two people can blend ... But the real work of two people blending—the behavior stuff—is where things really get interesting. Because after so many years of being by yourselves, no matter how much "Us" paint you throw on top of it, the old "You" still shows through.[1]

As we've explored the building blocks of marriage, enduring adult relationships allow two people to come together and create a loving, safe, and secure environment in which they can work through their unfinished business from the past and ultimately achieve wholeness. As author Joseph Barth once wrote, "Marriage is our last, best chance to grow up."[2]

As you and your partner struggle with completing unfinished business, you are at the same time designing, building, and maintaining a new couple relationship. Add to that your professional and work responsibilities, family obligations, friendships, and other social activities, and suddenly you've got a lot on your plate.

Underlying all of these responsibilities are your tangled webs of emotions, problems, conflicts, and connections to past experiences. And through each of these connections, your past beliefs and behaviors influence how you adapt to juggling your partner's wants, needs, expectations, and activities in addition to your own. In the midst of all of these conscious and unconscious transactions, you also want to sustain the blissfulness of being in love.

42

This is not an easy task. Yet, every year millions of people all over the world undertake this journey called marriage with the expectation of living happily ever after. Whenever a couple reaches the heavenly heights of love, however, they must inevitably come back down to earth and face the realities of life.

Fortunately, the natural cycles of our lives include a solid mix of pleasure with the work to be accomplished. This work also comes in manageable sizes and patterns that you can tackle step-by-step, building on your previous success.

Ideally, the marriage journey would progress in a predictable manner on a set schedule. Each stage would arrive with little fanfare on its previously appointed date and time. However, the length of a marriage is no real guide for what sort of issues a couple might face. Some couples may resolve some stages earlier than others, and some couples might be stuck in one place for years. In reality, self-discovery shuns clocks and calendars, and because you and your partner have different needs, you might not even be in the same stage at the same time.

I Want You to Want Me—I Need You to Need Me

Unfulfilled needs can appear in any stage in a marriage, but you must resolve them before either you or your partner can move into the next stage. These needs range from the most basic human necessities (food, water, air, touch, security) to the desire for love, affection, and belonging. In order for couples to fully embrace marriage, they must feel safe enough to reveal vulnerability without fear that their partners will use it to attack or manipulate them.

Beyond this, we all need to experience a sense of achievement and respect or appreciation. As you tackle each of the developmental tasks outlined in the following chapters, your success should fuel a sense of accomplishment and esteem. The couples who turn crises and transitions into opportunities for growth and change are far more motivated to work together in resolving their differences. Admiration and respect for their partners soar. Inspired by this success, they are then able to pursue their personal needs for knowledge, understanding, discovery, and beauty.

The trick with needs is that when you're by yourself, they don't seem all that selfish. They're just what you know you want and need. Your behavior doesn't really impact anyone else. But in a relationship, when you see those wants and needs bouncing back at you from another person, they may appear to be selfish, unrealistic, complex, and even contradictory.

You might have a strong need to belong—to be close and connected—while your partner may have an equally strong need to be independent and spend time alone. Neither need is inherently bad or wrong, just different. As a couple, you must find a reasonable way to meet both needs. Beyond your personal needs, your relationship has its own needs, and both people in the relationship bear responsibility for meeting them.

Each and every one of us has paradoxical needs to love and be loved; to nurture and be nurtured; to be cared for and to care for others; for security and for taking risks; for dependence and independence; for control and autonomy; and for being alone and belonging. We have needs for intimacy and for separateness as individuals, as a couple, and as parents.

Many of the developmental tasks outlined in the six stages of marriage revolve around the process of making room in our relationships for both individuals to experience themselves as whole people. The boundaries of your relationship should be flexible enough to allow both you and your partner to grow as individuals and as a couple. But how can two adults balance their paradoxical desires to live and love in harmony? A couple should view every struggle, every problem, and every conflict as an opportunity to learn—to learn about themselves and about each other—and be willing to share their thoughts, feelings, and needs openly and honestly.

The Six Stages of Marriage

Marriage isn't a static arrangement between two people. It's an adventure that "encourages empathetic separateness and continuously flowing rhythm of change."[3] In the following chapters, you'll discover the six stages of modern marriage:

1. Honeymoon
2. Expectation
3. Power struggle
4. Seven-year itch
5. Reconciliation
6. Acceptance

Although I developed this relationship model primarily for married couples, it is equally effective with almost any other enduring adult relationships including those of unmarried, cohabitating, and gay or lesbian couples, as well as those of remarried couples, business partners, coworkers, and friends.

In addition to an overview which describes the typical attitudes and behaviors related to each stage, the following chapters include segments devoted to:

Real Life
In this section, I provide glimpses into the lives of real couples designed to help you see yourself in one of these stages.

Taking Care of Business
Each stage includes a group of developmental tasks that need to be completed in order to transition into the next stage. Evelyn M. Duvall describes a developmental task as:

> one which arises at or about a certain period in the life of the individual, successful achievement of which leads to his happiness and to success with later tasks, while failure leads to unhappiness in the individual … and difficulty with later tasks.[4]

It boils down to this: if you complete the developmental tasks, you'll be able to move on with a happy and successful life. If you don't, you'll get stuck where you are until you do.

Getting Stuck
As you progress through the stages, your ability to master the developmental tasks of each depends on three things: (1) your environment; (2) your personality, temperament, and genetic background; and (3) your personal aspirations and values. Difficulties arise when you or your partner cannot master a task to progress to the next stage. This section outlines key indicators that you're stuck in a stage and how to proceed.

Marriage Tools
These segments outline the six essential interpersonal skills needed for a healthy relationship, including: communication, problem solving, conflict resolution, negotiation, forgiveness, and maintenance (of love, empathy, respect, and caring). I also provide step-by-step instructions for developing and mastering these skills.

Do Try This at Home
All new skills require practice. These exercises will help you apply the tools of marriage to current situations in your relationship.

Moving On
With the exception of death or divorce, the journey of marriage is a continuous process. Although the stages fall into six neat categories, real life does not. Our personal growth doesn't usually proceed in a linear fashion from one stage to the next. When you hit stress at any point in the relationship, it's easy to fall back to an earlier stage if the issues that trigger the stress are denied or repressed on the first time through. This section is a guide to transition you from one stage to the next, bringing you closer to a happy, healthy relationship.

The Great Adventure

Here then is the crux of marital growth and development: at its center, every marriage is an adventure during which two partners struggle to achieve balance between the strivings for dependence and independence and closeness and distance and to ultimately achieve a mutually intimate relationship. As Rilke once wrote, "For one human being to love another human being: that is perhaps the most difficult task that has been entrusted to us, the ultimate task, the final test and proof, the work for which all other work is merely preparation."[5]

The thought of peeling back the layers of your love and your life is probably somewhat intimidating. Most people worry about how they will feel, whether or not they can change, or what other people might think. But the results are worth it. This is your map. Are you ready?

Stage One: The Honeymooners

ɼ hon•ey•moon
Pronunciation: \ hə-nē-mün\
Function: *noun*
Date: 1546
Etymology: from the idea that the first month of marriage is the sweetest
Definition: a period of harmony immediately following marriage[1]

Do you remember when you fell in love? You probably couldn't go more than a few minutes without thinking about your beloved. You lay awake at night replaying your conversations in your head. You probably drove through a red light or two. Every love song seemed written just for you. You couldn't keep your hands off of each other. It was easy to love this perfect person who would spend the rest of his or her life providing for your wants, your needs, and your happiness.

This highly romanticized, idealized, and exclusive relationship is what I call the "honeymoon stage." I am not referring to the romantic getaway enjoyed by the bride and groom shortly after the wedding. I am referring to a period of time in which the rosy glow of romance minimizes the couple's differences and accentuates their similarities to the point that the partners seem to share the same values, interests, habits, thoughts, feelings, and ideas. *We are one. We are the same. You are perfect. I am yours, and you are mine.*

Falling in love and connecting deeply requires a couple to come together, establish a boundary around each other, and retreat into the pleasures of the relationship. This merging, exclusivity, and regression are critical factors in developing a sense of belonging and trust in the relationship.

Real Life

I had intended to include a real-life example of a couple experiencing the stage described in each chapter. But the truth is that couples rarely come to therapy during the honeymoon stage, even if they should. The delirious joy of love numbs their sensibilities to the inevitable challenges faced by two people merging two lives into one marriage.

While the honeymoon stage is often a time of intense romance and pleasure, the developmental tasks undertaken during this stage are typically more complex then the ecstatic couple may realize. Most newlyweds enter into marriage believing that love conquers all and that they will live happily ever after. They expect happiness to be an automatic byproduct of marriage. But from the moment they decide to move forward with the relationship, every couple must learn how to balance not only the social and cultural expectations of marriage but also the individual hopes, needs, and desires that ultimately affect the marriage relationship.[2]

Taking Care of Business

Psychologists have different opinions as to the length of the honeymoon stage. Some say it lasts between six and nine months, while others claim that it can continue for up to three years. In my years of private practice and research, I have discovered that transitions in marriage don't adhere to a preset schedule. Time, in terms of psychological development, doesn't abide by the calendar. I have met a couple whose honeymoon stage lasted only a few days, while another couple claimed to be honeymooning thirty years into their marriage. Couples should use the honeymoon stage, regardless of its length, to build the foundation for a mutually satisfying, caring, and supportive marriage relationship that is separate from their families of origin. Let's take a closer look at the four developmental tasks that couples face in the honeymoon stage.

1. Cut the Apron Strings

When you enter into a marriage relationship, you must begin to relinquish your family of origin as your primary sources of love and gratification and turn to your couple relationship to meet those needs. Cutting the apron strings doesn't mean that you abandon your family or cut them out of your life completely. What it does mean is that your marriage replaces your family as the central relationship in your life as Nathan and Elaine discover in the vignette below.

> Nathan came to his first therapy session about four years into his marriage to Elaine. "I don't know what to do anymore," he said in frustration. "I feel useless and unimportant in my marriage. I don't even know why I'm still here."

Nathan and Elaine resemble a lot of couples that I've met over the years. They have a lot in common and enjoy many of the same activities. They have good jobs, are doing okay financially, and were able to buy a house soon after they were married. And yet, Nathan was depressed and thinking about leaving his young wife.

In looking back over their four years of marriage, it didn't take long for Nathan to figure out why he felt inadequate. Whenever he and Elaine needed something expensive, Elaine turned to her parents instead of to him. "When we moved into our house and needed to buy a refrigerator, she hinted about it to her mom, and the next thing you know, a fridge was delivered to the house," he explained. When he asked Elaine why she hadn't discussed this with him, she said that her parents didn't mind getting things for her because she was their only child, and they were happy to help out. More recently, Elaine's father had purchased new tires for her car when she complained that her old ones were getting thin.

By turning to her parents for things that she assumed she and Nathan couldn't afford, Elaine was clinging to her family of origin for financial support rather than sharing her desires with her husband. Her failure to cut the apron strings left Nathan feeling unimportant, inadequate, and useless.

Making your marriage your primary relationship is a process that takes time, but it's a process that is vital to the future of your marriage. If a couple fails to make the marriage their primary relationship, one or both partners will begin to feel useless and look elsewhere (to their family, their job, an affair, a hobby, an addiction) for the love, gratification, and support that should come from a spouse.

Nathan and Elaine's situation also points out that newlyweds aren't the only ones who might have difficulty cutting the apron strings. Some parents resist their child's efforts to form a new family. Perhaps that's why the world suffers from an abundance of in-law jokes. Today, adult children tend to live at home longer and marry later than in previous generations. Life is also more expensive than it was in the past, and many couples rely on their families for childcare or financial support in the early years of marriage. Adult children also play an important role in caring for their aging parents. These circumstances make it easier for both parties to cling to the parent-child relationship that existed before the marriage. You often hear wedding toasts where proud parents beam at the newlywed couple and say, "We haven't lost a daughter/son; we've gained a son/daughter." The truth, however, is that through their children's marriages, parents do give up their child as an individual. They must relinquish the primary parent-child relationship in order to welcome the adult child and his or her partner back into the family as a married couple.

As a couple, your families will always be a part of your lives, and you will always be a part of your families. The key to cutting the apron strings is to establish relationship boundaries that enable you to interact with the world around you while still preserving your marriage as your primary relationship.

②. Establish Relationship Boundaries

As you develop your couple identity, you will need to establish boundaries that shelter your marriage relationship from outside influences. Even for couples who have lived together before the wedding, marriage changes the boundaries of the relationship. Therefore, it is important to establish clear guidelines and make sure that everyone involved knows where those boundaries are.

This can be a difficult thing to do. Both you and your partner have years of history with your families of origin but relatively less history with each other. It's easy for feelings of guilt or obligation to pull you both in different directions. Where will you spend the holidays? Who is welcome in your home? How will you spend and save your money? Will spirituality be an important part of your relationship? This is the time to decide which aspects of your relationship you will share with other people and which parts you will reserve for just the two of you. Sex, money, and in-laws are the three leading causes of marital stress, and most of that stress boils down to boundary issues. Take some time now to develop the guidelines that will be your support when the honeymoon is over and real life begins.

In order to build relationship boundaries, couples should ask questions similar to the following:

- What values and beliefs are important to us as individuals and as a couple?
  Answers to this question can help you determine where to devote the bulk of your time, money, and energy.

_____

_____

_____

- Who are the important people in our lives? What roles did they play in the past and how will those roles change now that we are married? Answers to these questions can help you set guidelines for when, where, and in what situations you spend time or share information with other people.

_____

_____

_____

_____

- How will we balance our time between our marriage, our families, our careers, our friends, and our own interests? Answers to this question can help you establish healthy boundaries while still letting each person express their own needs for personal and professional growth.

_____

_____

_____

_____

With each of these questions, ask yourself about the boundaries in your family of origin.

- Were they comfortable for you?
- Are they similar or different to those experienced by your partner?
- How will you accommodate those differences in your relationship?

The answers to these questions can provide you with a starting point for developing the boundaries of your marriage.

In *Anna Karenina*, Leo Tolstoy wrote, "There are as many minds as there are heads, so there are as many kinds of love as there are hearts." The same is true of relationships. There are as many kinds of relationships as there are couples.

In all of my years as a therapist, I've never seen two couples approach their relationship in exactly the same way. Each couple must develop its own method together.

3. Remember Who You Are

When you flip through a magazine, search the self-help section of the bookstore, or surf your television channels, it doesn't take long to realize that almost everybody has an opinion on how to behave in a marriage. While there are hundreds of opinions as to the proper roles of husbands and wives, you ultimately have to decide for yourselves what each partner's role will be within your relationship. Who will cook and clean? Who will pay the bills? Will both of you work? Will you have children? When?

Everybody enters into marriage with conscious and unconscious expectations based on past experiences and cultural influences. In the early days of the honeymoon stage, it's easy to imagine that you'll never argue. But you will. Take some time during the honeymoon stage to explore the different roles that each of you hold within your relationship.

Even though a marriage consists of two people, it contains four separate relationships: man and woman, man and wife, husband and woman, husband and wife.

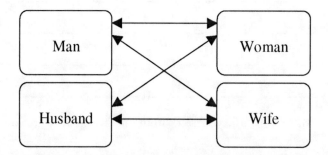

Therefore, you must learn to relate to your spouse not only as part of a new couple relationship, but also as an individual with unique talents, tastes, and opinions. While marriage changes how you relate to each other in many ways, the relationship should not strip either of you of your own identity.

To get an understanding of the different roles influencing your marriage, take a few minutes to develop a list of all of the roles that make up each of your lives.

Partner A	Spheres of Influence	Partner B
	Self (man/woman)	
	Marriage (husband/wife)	
	Family (father/mother/son/daugh- ter/brother/sister)	
	Extended Family (uncle/aunt/cousin/grand- child/grandparent)	
	Career (employer/employee)	
	Community (volunteer/church member/leader/etc.)	
	Friendships	
	Other	

Hopefully, looking over this list will help you see the complex web of relationships that each person brings into a marriage. By working through these roles together, you can prioritize them in the way that best suits the needs of your relationship. Don't forget that some of these roles and responsibilities will change throughout the course of your marriage, so it's a good idea to discuss them periodically to make sure that your patterns are still working for both of you.

One way to rediscover your partner's individuality after marriage is to continue the dating process. Young lovers spend countless hours talking about anything and everything, including their pasts, their dreams, their preferences, their childhood pets. You name it; they talk about it. This practice of sharing should continue after marriage.

Daily Dozen

I recommend that couples spend twenty minutes a day and one evening a week "dating" each other. Take a walk, browse through a bookstore, or go bowling. I know of one couple who went on a date to the grocery store. They spent an evening wandering through the aisles and talking about different things they liked to eat and how different foods reminded them of events and celebrations from their pasts. I also recommend that couples go away overnight every six to eight weeks to spend devoted time together, uninterrupted by the other relationships in their lives. *(once a quarter)*

*   *   *

Marriage Tool #1: Communication

Have you ever noticed that what you say and what your partner hears isn't always the same? Miscommunication is often at the root of both our simplest and most complex conflicts. Markman, Stanley, and Blumberg's research indicates that the two major predictors of marital success are communication and conflict resolution.[3] If you're aiming for a marriage that lasts a lifetime, refining your communication skills is a great place to start.

The word "communication" comes from the Latin *communicare* meaning "to impart, share, or make common."[4] Its key root is *mun-*, which also shows up in *mun*ificent and com*mun*ity. Webster defines communication as "a process by which information is exchanged between individuals through a common system of symbols, signs, or behavior."[5]

Communication includes verbal and nonverbal language: our spoken and unspoken thoughts, gestures, facial expressions, and feelings. Everything about us as human beings, from what we say to how we dress, sends a message. Therefore, we cannot *not* communicate. After all, even silence is a form of communication. Effective communication in a relationship is based on the following guidelines:

- Express your thoughts, feelings, ideas, and beliefs openly and honestly.

- Make "I" statements rather than "you" statements.

- Maintain eye contact and speak clearly.
- Listen attentively.
- Acknowledge the communication that you receive without evaluation or judgment.
- Give and receive accurate and honest feedback.

We give feedback in order to express understanding of, non-understanding of, agreement with, or disagreement with the communication that we receive. Feedback also validates or negates our assumptions and allows us to share in the effect and outcome of the message. Actions that destroy effective communication include:

- Making assumptions
- Not listening
- Preparing your reply while the other person is still talking
- Arguing
- Withdrawing
- Blaming and accusing
- Changing the subject

What makes communication within a relationship difficult is that each of us comes from a family with its own communication system. When couples come together, they need to examine and even break down their existing systems in order to create a new communication pattern that works for both people. This is one of the most important tools of marriage because effective communication skills will help to decrease future conflict. Establishing good communication skills takes a lot of practice, and that is why twenty-minute daily dates are so important. Daily periods of affirmation and acceptance are essential for a healthy marriage.

*   *   *

4. Develop a Satisfying Level of Intimacy

Although it may not seem like it during the honeymoon stage, there's more to intimacy than sex. And, as with almost every other aspect of marriage, perceptions from your family of origin will influence how you and your partner approach intimacy. Some families are very open about physical affection; others are more reserved. Some families encourage their children to save sex for marriage; others do not. The honeymoon stage is the time to lay the groundwork for an appropriate and mutually satisfying level of intimacy with your spouse.

Much like happiness, intimacy is not a guaranteed result of reciting marriage vows. In 1854, Henry David Thoreau wrote, "The mass of men lead lives of quiet desperation." Over 150 years later, little has changed. A large majority of divorced women claim that their married years were the loneliest of their lives, and 84 percent of women feel that they don't experience intimacy (oneness) in their marriages.[6]

Intimacy requires authenticity between two people who genuinely desire to become closer to each other. In describing intimacy, Steven Korch writes, "It is both moving toward another and likewise allowing that person the freedom to approach. It brings the delightful experience of sharing personal space in the midst of a very private and alienated world."[7]

Developing intimacy and a satisfying sex life within marriage requires you to put aside your pre-wired gender differences, family history, sexual history, personal preferences, and expectations in order to honestly communicate the deepest desires of your heart.

Actor John Barrymore described sex as "the thing that takes up the least amount of time and causes the most amount of trouble." He's not far off the mark. The expectations that follow us into the bedroom can set the stage for years of pleasure or years of disappointment. Achieving true intimacy is one of life's great risks because those whom we love the most have the ability to wound us most deeply. But when nurtured within a loving relationship, intimacy's rewards are unmatched by any other experience or feeling.

Getting Stuck

Family therapy literature describes couples who are stuck in the honeymoon stage as being enmeshed, merged, or undifferentiated. Some characteristics of these couples include:

- An emphasis on the word "we" rather than "I," implying that both partners have the exact same thoughts, feelings, and values
- A tendency for one partner to cling very closely to the other resulting in "emotional flooding" as one partner is devastated by the other's attempts to create a unique identity
- A tendency for one partner to exhibit high abandonment anxiety while the other may feel smothered or experience high engulfment anxiety

- Little or no capacity to see each other as separate individuals
- A fear of discovering that they might have differences
- A lack of problem-solving and negotiation skills

These couples are unable to function as individuals and will eventually smother each other until one person goes crazy, has an affair, or leaves the relationship. In describing the nature of the "pure relationship" of the honeymoon stage, Anne Morrow Lindbergh writes:

> One comes in the end to realize that there is no permanent pure-relationship and there should not be. It is not even something to be desired. The pure relationship is limited, in space and in time. In its essence it implies exclusion. It excludes the rest of life, other relationships, other sides of personality, other responsibilities, other possibilities in the future. It excludes growth.[8]

Indeed, to remain in this stage indefinitely is to forfeit your individuality for a lifetime of dependency.

Do Try This at Home: Communication

Take some time away from your partner to answer the questions below. Then set aside some time to come together as a couple to discuss your answers. As you do, practice some of the communication tips provided in the Marriage Toolbox. Remember to be open to listening, hearing, and sharing points of view.

1. What was your family structure like?
    - Who came into the family?
    - Who left the family?
    - How did these changes affect you?

_____

_____

_____

_____

_____

_____

2. How did your parents set boundaries and priorities in their relationship?
   • What was important to your family?
   • How did you carry out those values?
   • How did your family handle success and failure?

   _____

   _____

   _____

   _____

   _____

3. How did you see your parents carry out the roles of husband and wife?
   • What impressed you the most about their relationship?
   • What impressed you the least?
   • How did they have fun?

   _____

   _____

   _____

   _____

   _____

4. What did you learn about intimacy and sex in your family?
    - How did your family express affection?
    - How did your family respect each other's privacy?

    _____

    _____

    _____

    _____

    _____

    _____

5. How did your parents communicate?
    - How did they relate to each other and to their children?
    - How did they handle feelings of sorrow, joy, anger, grief, happiness, etc.?
    - How did they solve problems and deal with conflicts?
    - Did they disagree? Reconcile? Express forgiveness?

    _____

    _____

    _____

    _____

    _____

    _____

Hopefully these questions will illustrate that although the euphoria of love may have smoothed over your differences, you are in fact individual people with different perceptions and experiences. And that's okay. When partners realize that they aren't exactly alike, the honeymoon is over, and the real foundation of the marriage is ready for construction.

Moving On

Author Lisa Moriyama says, "If a relationship is to evolve, it must go through a series of endings." The transition out of the honeymoon stage is one such ending.

Transition times are the most difficult and least stable points in a relationship, and it is during these transition periods when most couples end up in my office. Personal growth is painful and frequently meets a great deal of resistance from one or both partners. This is where the rollercoaster that is marriage really begins.

When you begin to relinquish the blissful fantasy of perfection and experience differences, you are transitioning into the expectation stage. This transition begins when one person starts to differentiate from their partner. They may want to pursue an independent activity or express an opposing opinion. Although this is a natural progression within a healthy relationship, disappointment and disillusionment usually surface as the other partner attempts to hold on to their similarities for as long as possible.

Because one of the unconscious purposes for getting married is to recapture the unconditional love of early childhood, this first period of rejection within the marriage relationship can be quite a shock. But as Maxine Rock points out, "people who cling desperately to the fantasy and keep trying to force their mates to act like parents will eventually erode the relationships."[9]

Stage Two: Great Expectations

Infatuation is when you think that he's as sexy as Robert Redford,
as smart as Henry Kissinger, as noble as Ralph Nader,
as funny as Woody Allen, and as athletic as Jimmy Conners.
Love is when you realize that he's as sexy as Woody Allen,
as smart as Jimmy Conners, as funny as Ralph Nader,
as athletic as Henry Kissinger, and nothing like Robert Redford
—but you'll take him anyway.
~ Judith Viorst

As blissful as the honeymoon stage may be, every couple ultimately comes face to face with the reality of marriage: while a marriage consists of one couple, that couple is made up of two separate people. Both people are unique individuals with different tastes, opinions, and experiences, and each comes from a unique family of origin with its own set of expectations as to what it means to be a husband or a wife. At this point in the marriage journey, the complexities of daily life, a commitment to careers, or the possible arrival of children alert the couple to the fact that they may not see eye to eye on as many issues as they originally thought.

During the honeymoon stage, both partners usually experience sexual fulfillment and an intense feeling of closeness, as if they are one. With these initial needs satisfied, however, one partner is usually ready to move on to the next stage. If the other partner isn't ready to let go of those intense feelings of oneness, disappointment creeps into the relationship. Although the couple might try to accommodate this shift as one partner moves toward more independence, they usually end up struggling to maintain harmony using whatever strategies necessary.

Even though this is typically the first major period of conflict within the marriage, it is my experience that few couples seek help at this point. Perhaps that is why we see so many marriages in their early stages ending in divorce these days. At the first feelings of disillusionment or disappointment, one partner simply decides that their differences are irreconcilable and opts for divorce. It doesn't have to end that way.

Real Life: Chris and Jenni

Chris and Jenni wound up in my office after three years of marriage. In our session, I began to see signs of disillusionment and asked Jenni to tell me about her first disappointment of the marriage. Bursting into tears, Jenni sobbed, "It was our honeymoon."

Jenni had wanted to honeymoon in Hawaii, but Chris thought it was too expensive. He went ahead and arranged a beach vacation that was closer to home and less expensive, which left Jenni feeling hurt and disappointed.

During one of their sessions, Jenni was finally able to express her disappointment. Chris was thoroughly surprised. He thought that she had been on board with his more practical honeymoon plan. In return, Chris was able to reveal his own disappointment in the fact that Jenni was more frivolous with money than he was. Within the span of a few sessions, they decided to plan a second honeymoon to Hawaii, and several weeks later, I received this postcard:

"Having a wonderful time. Thank you!"

Like Chris and Jenni, many couples allow early disappointments to set the tone for their marriage. With the right tools, however, couples can change their behavioral patterns early on and lay the foundation for an enduring and intimate relationship.

Taking Care of Business

The realization that you and your partner really are different takes time to negotiate and requires you to explore how your families handled differentness, differences, and rules about disagreements. The expectations that each of you bring into your relationship usually derive from your parents' relationship models or cultural influences such as magazines, television, and movies. However, in order to fit into the roles necessary to achieve your mutual goals and fulfill the responsibilities of your relationships, each of you must be able to change or reconcile your expectations. Let's take a closer look at the five developmental tasks that couples face in the expectation stage.

1. Say Good-Bye to the All-Encompassing Lover

What happens when Prince Charming turns out to be Prince Irksome? When you realize that your partner isn't perfect, you will need to release any lingering fantasies of your partner as an all-encompassing lover who will fulfill all of your needs. Your personal fulfillment, even in a marriage relationship, cannot be solely dependent on your partner. While a spouse can play a large role in helping to fulfill some needs (such as the needs for closeness, a sense of belonging, or a caring relationship), you are ultimately the only one who can meet your own needs. Therefore, as you become aware of your differences, you will need to establish new patterns of relating to each other.

> *James and Angela came to see me in their sixth year of marriage because James was concerned about Angela's distant and preoccupied behavior. She was also no longer interested in having a child. After six months of meeting separately with me, Angela confessed that she had been fantasizing about a former lover. She couldn't get him off of her mind and often wondered how he was doing, what he looked like, and if she had made a mistake in letting him go. Ultimately, she decided to return to her hometown to see him.*
>
> *When she arrived at our next session, she was filled with disappointment. Her former lover in no way lived up to her fantasies of him. She was clearly disillusioned with her supposed Prince Charming. After confronting her fantasies, Angela was able to see the truth about her husband—that he was a wonderful, caring, and supportive man—and she stayed with the marriage even while she unraveled her fantasies.*

Like Angela, many people have difficulty letting go of idealized fantasy partners, whether they are past lovers or the current spouse. In order to embrace your differences, however, you must face them head on. If you (or your partner) are at a point in your relationship where you need to let go of your fantasies and expectations, you must first acknowledge that you are indeed creating a fantasy partner in your own mind.

To refocus attention on the positive aspects of your partner, try some of the following ideas:

- On a sheet of paper, devote one side to writing out your fantasies and expectations about your partner. On the other side of the page, describe in detail the real person (differences and all).

- Place a picture of your partner in a place where you will see it often. Examine that picture every time you see it to remember what attracted you to that person when you first met.

- Spend time with your partner reminiscing about your first meeting or your first dates. Tell each other what your thoughts and feelings were during those events and what memories stand out to you now.

- You can even spend time discussing your first disappointments in the relationship, and encourage your partner to do likewise.

Sharing what may be unspoken parts of your relationship will give you an opportunity to clear the air and your heads and enable you to focus on the real aspects of the relationship that the two of you are building together. Setting aside a regular time when you can discuss where you've been and where you're going can relieve hidden tensions within the relationship and create an opportunity to share your hopes, fears, and plans for the future.

2. See Yourselves as Husband and Wife

When conflicts arising from different styles and expectations creep into a marriage, it is easy to slip into a parent/child behavior pattern with one spouse monitoring, chastising, or punishing the behavior of the other. Differences and expectations need to be handled within the husband/wife relationship with each of you having the freedom to express your wants, needs, and desires without the fear of punishment or retaliation.

To change the parent/child pattern, you must first be aware of its existence. In many cases, couples don't even realize when they have slipped into this destructive pattern, especially if they saw their own parents interact in a similar way.

One of my client couples fell into this pattern over the arrangement of their kitchen.

Michael was at least ten years older than Michelle when she married him at the age of nineteen. He claims that at the time "Michelle didn't even know how to boil water" and that he taught her everything she knew about cooking and keeping house. Michelle agreed that Michael had taught her a lot, but now she wanted to rearrange the kitchen, and he wouldn't let her.

When I asked her how this made her feel, she immediately responded, "Like a child! I may have been young and inexperienced when we married, but I've learned a lot in the past ten years." Michael was hurt by Michelle's desire for more independence, claiming that he felt "pushed out" as if she didn't need him anymore.

Michael had done a great job of parenting his wife, and initially she responded well to his teaching. After ten years of marriage, however, they needed to strike a more adult balance in their relationship. At first, Michael was reluctant to agree to the changes, but after talking through Michelle's ideas, he agreed that they could still work together. They did rearrange the kitchen, and they also took some time to rearrange their relationship, moving out of the parent/child pattern and reestablishing themselves as two adults in a husband/wife relationship.

3. Establish the Rules of Your Relationship

Each couple relationship is unique in that its particular combination of individuals is a once-in-a-lifetime experience. It's unrealistic to think that there is a predetermined pattern to marriage into which a couple must mold their relationship. You and your partner bring multiple roles into your marriage—those of husband/wife, son/daughter, employee, friend, sibling, parent—that shake up the mix. You also both have unique talents and skills. Therefore, each new marriage requires its own unique set of rules that establish the boundaries and roles of the relationship.

Differences and expectations take time to negotiate, but a review of your families of origin will go a long way to reveal how each of you learned to handle differences and what expectations are already ingrained in your understanding of the marriage relationship. In many cases, your parents served as your model of what to expect in the roles of husband and wife. But the roles that your parents created for themselves may not work for your relationship. You must be willing to reconcile or change your preconceived ideas, if necessary, to achieve the goals and fulfill the responsibilities within the new relationship.

As you review your families of origin, ask yourselves the following questions:

- How did I see my parents handle various tasks like household chores, money, in-laws, disciplining children, making plans, etc.?

● How did Mom and Dad communicate when they experienced difficulties?

_____

_____

● How did they ultimately solve the problem?

_____

_____

Using the answers to these questions, you and your partner (possibly with the help of a therapist) can begin to explore, without judgment or blame, your perceptions of marriage. Most likely, you will begin to see similarities in your own patterns of behavior.

> After eight years of marriage, John and Sarah came to see me on the verge of separation. Sarah was determined, saying, "I'm the one who lit this fire. I'm thirty years old. We've been married for eight years, and I don't like my life as it is. He gets hostile and walks out but then comes back later and pretends that things are back to normal. That's where we stay. He won't change, and I want a separation."

> John admitted that the couple has had communication problems for the past two years. "In arguments, I'm always trying to be right," he explained. "It's difficult for me to admit that there might be a different way to deal with problems." He also admitted that for the past year and a half he has indulged in partying and staying out all night.

In the case of John and Sarah, a review of their families of origin gave them a foundation to better understand their expectations and behaviors within their relationship.

> John's parents are in their late sixties and have been married for thirty-five years. They frequently fought about money. Both of his parents held irregular jobs, and neither was the main breadwinner. When his parents fought, he would hide in his room and cry, always threatened by the pos-

sibility of divorce. As there was little money, John went to work at a very young age. His parents did not show much affection toward each other or toward John and his younger brother. Sadly, John says that he never had much of a relationship with his dad, and while he spent more time with his mother, they weren't that close. In fact, John feels neglected by both of his parents.

Sarah had few memories of her early childhood, but she does remember that her mother always worked hard and that her father spent much of his time away on business. Sarah got in trouble a lot in her teen years, particularly by running away, only to be grounded when she returned. Although her father reduced his working hours during her adolescence to spend more time at home, Sarah claims, "He didn't know how to show affection or talk to me. He was just home more than he had been before."

After reviewing their family histories, John and Sarah began to recognize the source of their poor communication and tendency to argue without resolving any issues. Their parents had been unable to resolve any of their issues and therefore didn't pass on the ability to do so to their children, who then repeated the pattern in their own relationships. Sarah also realized that running away as a teenager was an attempt to get her father's attention and that she was repeating that process with John by asking for a separation.

Equipped with a better understanding of their behavioral patterns, John and Sarah are now much more able to handle them. Over time, they stopped blaming each other for their problems and focused their attention on improving their communication skills and spending time with their two children. In changing their own destructive patterns, they hope to save their children from repeating the same mistakes in the future.

As you establish the rules and boundaries that work for your relationship, you will be able to deal with conflict and tension much more effectively while remaining connected.

④ Reconcile Your Differences

In many cases, couples in the early stages of marriage maintain harmony and deal with disagreements through techniques that resemble denial, distortion, deception, or misperception. Avoiding conflict in an effort to prolong the honeymoon stage is a common occurrence, but where avoidance is the chosen method for dealing with conflict, the relationship takes on a static quality with no sense of movement or growth.

In order to achieve adult goals and fulfill responsibilities within the marriage, you and your partner must learn how to actively reconcile or accept your differences. You need to learn how to compromise—to give up some of your own demands or make concessions in order to reach a settlement. In order to compromise, therefore, both of you need to have a clear understanding of the differences at hand and an ability to clearly state those differences. In other cases, you may need to agree to disagree.

Oftentimes, couples fall back on the methods of problem-solving modeled by their parents. I see many cases where one parent made all of the rules and decisions while the other complied. Other couples saw their parents work through problems at the kitchen table, ultimately reaching an agreement.

*   *   *

Marriage Tool #2: Problem Solving

Problem-solving is a step-by-step process that focuses on the problem—one problem at a time—and not on the personality of the people in conflict. Consider these steps as you work through your differences and practice the art of compromise:

- **Define the problem.** Make sure that you both understand the issue at stake and are working toward the same goal.

- **List all possible solutions.** This will ensure that you have considered all possible options and give you a record of your ideas for the future.

- **Select one solution that is agreeable to both partners.** You may not get everything you want, but be sure to select a solution that you can both live with.

- **Select a time to review the outcome.** Review the original problem, and determine whether the solution is producing the expected results in a way that is mutually acceptable to both of you.

- **Select another solution.** If you are not satisfied with the outcome of your first solution, don't be afraid to try something else. Nothing is set in stone.

- **Celebrate resolutions.** When the problem is solved, reward each other. Find a way to commemorate and celebrate your accomplishment.

* * *

5. Create Space within the Relationship

During the expectation stage, either you begin or your partner begins to desire more space than you required during the honeymoon stage. You may crave time alone to pursue personal interests or to begin to reconnect with family members, friends, and coworkers who were neglected during the intense close-ness of the honeymoon stage. It is both healthy and beneficial to the relation-ship for you to have personal space within the relationship, provided that your activities fall within the boundaries set by the rules of the relationship.

In order to create that space within the relationship, consider each other's wants and needs. Does she need an evening out with her girlfriends? Does he want to watch a few games with the guys? If you never saw your parents spend-ing time apart pursuing individual interests or going out with friends, you may cling to an underlying belief that cultivating other friendships isn't permitted within the boundaries of marriage.

A family of origin review can also be helpful if either of you experience or express a fear of solitude or of pursuing separate activities and friendships. In these situations, I look for early childhood experiences that limited indepen-dence and may have instilled a fear of punishment that now holds you back as an adult. Working through those fears will enable you to be more assertive while still being accepted for the person you are now.

In either situation, if either of you live by the rule "we must do everything together," then that rule needs to change in order for the marriage to thrive.

In the case of John and Sarah (discussed in the previous section), they decided that they needed to find more constructive ways of spending time alone and developing individual interests. John's all-night partying bouts came to an end, and Sarah took on a part-time job. In exchange, John spends time with the children on the evenings that Sarah works.

Getting Stuck

If you fail to complete these five developmental tasks, your relationship will fizzle out in the expectation stage. When couples get stuck in this stage, one partner usually tries to coerce the other to come back into the former state of oneness that was enjoyed during the honeymoon stage. That partner may beg, plead, and even threaten, while the other may initially attempt to accommodate the partner's desires but eventually wind up feeling angry or resentful. In other cases, the partner who differentiates first may try to explain his or her desires and encourage the other to pursue his or her own interests and friendships, only to be accused of covering up for or wanting to have an affair. The relationship becomes very stressful as one partner moves forward while the other holds back and becomes entrenched in his or her position and unwilling or unable to let go.

Do Try This at Home: Problem-Solving

Take some time away from your partner to answer the following questions. Then set aside some time to come together as a couple to discuss your answers. As you do, you will be able to determine the degree of autonomy that your relationship can currently tolerate.

1. Do you spend time pursuing activities away from your partner? If so, how often? If not, why not?

   _____

   _____

   _____

   _____

2. How comfortable are you with doing things away from your partner?

   _____

   _____

   _____

3. How comfortable are you with your partner doing things away from you?

   _____

   _____

_____

_____

4. What do you find most fulfilling about your relationship?

    _____

    _____

    _____

    _____

5. What do you find least fulfilling about your relationship?

    _____

    _____

    _____

    _____

6. In what significant ways are you similar to your partner?

    _____

    _____

    _____

    _____

7. In what significant ways are you different from your partner?

    _____

    _____

    _____

    _____

8. What methods have you developed as a couple to accommodate or resolve your differences?

_____

_____

_____

_____

As you share your answers with your partner, be open to listening, hearing, and sharing points of view.

If, at this point, one of you still desires to do everything together and feels hurt or abandoned by your partner's individual activities, it is quite possible that there are more deep-seated problems than mere differences of opinion or a need for space. I would recommend that you seek outside help individually or as a couple to get to the root of the problem.

Moving On

When you are able to recognize and affirm one another's individuality, you are ready to transition out of the expectation stage. This transition takes time. I have come to understand that as you reach a new level of understanding and compromise, you are often able to recognize when you slip back into your old patterns of behavior. This gives you time to correct your slip-ups and continue working on developing the new behaviors. As you gain confidence and strength in this part of the individuation process, you will begin to move toward the next stage, which often starts when a relationship takes a painful or difficult turn. As people, we rarely stay the same for very long. Just when we start to feel confident with life, life happens.

Stage Three: The Power Struggle

The course of true love never did run smooth.
~ William Shakespeare
(*A Midsummer Night's Dream*)

People get married and then they do the most hideous,
unbelievable things to each other.
~ Nicholas Cage as Jack Singer
(*Honeymoon in Vegas*)

I can recognize a couple trapped in a power struggle from the moment they walk through my office door. Their coldness, distance, and pain fill up the silence. Finally, one shrugs and states the obvious: "We're not getting along. We fight all the time. We can't agree on anything."

During the honeymoon stage, partners focus their effort on building intimacy and nurturing their new relationship. During the expectation stage, they realize how different they really are in the ways that they think, feel, work, communicate, and complete tasks. They also realize that they need time apart from each other to be alone or with friends, family, or coworkers. Gradually, they move out of their cocoon-like existence and expand the boundaries of their relationship to include other people and activities.

As the couple moves into the power struggle stage, their focus shifts again. One or both people begin to wonder: *Can I really be myself in this relationship? Will my partner still love me if I express how I really feel? What if I want to do something my way? What if I disagree? Will I be accepted?*

To find the answers to these questions, they begin to test the waters. One person may tug in one direction only to find that his or her partner is pulling in a different direction. Arguments erupt over seemingly insignificant decisions like which movie to see, how to fold the laundry, or what to have for dinner. A little while later, the couple looks back on these disruptions and wonders what all of the fuss was about.

While these arguments seem insignificant on the surface, a power struggle is usually brewing underneath. The relationship has become a testing ground in which each partner wants to experiment with taking control.

The battle to resolve the issue of who is in charge of or responsible for what can take on a variety of forms: silence, withdrawal, ambivalence, distrust, anger, blame, emotional tug-of-war, polarization, and even verbal or physical abuse. As each partner sheds inhibitions and lets his or her true self emerge, the relationship dissolves into chaos.

The most common complaints of couples in this stage are: "We can't communicate" and "We don't understand each other anymore." The more demands that one partner expresses, the more likely they are to view the partner's reaction as stubborn, unreasonable, emotional, or illogical. This cycle merely escalates the temptation to blame the conflict on the other person.

Both partners feel confused, hurt, alone, and scared, wondering why the love of their life no longer desires to make them happy. The real issue, however, isn't one of happiness but one of control. Neither person knows how to reach the other without surrendering their own wants and desires. They both view compromise as a surrender of identity, control, and newly found power. Chaos ensues as the couple struggles to balance individual identities with the couple relationship.

The power struggle is an intimate dance of approach and withdrawal. The pain is immense, but neither partner will allow him or herself to be vulnerable in such a threatening situation. *Can I be myself? Should I give in or fight on? Will I lose myself or my partner? What will I gain?*

For two people who love each other, the situation is contradictory. In order to be accepted, each partner must be open, honest, and vulnerable with the other. At the same time, that vulnerability increases the risk of rejection. It is a risk to show someone the aspects of one's true self when it is so much easier to control or overpower that person in order to get one's own way. It is a risk to reveal personal vulnerability while desiring empathy, love, and understanding in return.

To avoid this risk, however, is to be stuck in an unending battle over who's right and who's wrong—over who will win and who will lose. At best, these battles create distance between couples. At their worst, they destroy any semblance of love and trust. Couples trapped in a power struggle are some of the most wounded people on earth.

Real Life: Allen and Kathleen

Allen and Kathleen are engaged in a classic power struggle over money. Kathleen is a saver, and Allen is a spender. Kathleen's frugal father didn't waste a dime and taught his children to save. "The theme of our life was, 'Don't spend money,'" explained Kathleen. "We practically had to beg for money to do anything fun." In her own marriage, Kathleen is meticulous about money.

Allen, on the other hand, is a terrific spender. "We grew up on a limited income, so when I started earning my own money, I knew I wanted to spend it on things that I would enjoy," he said. Together, they make a good living, but Kathleen wants Allen to save his money for retirement so that they can travel and do things they've always wanted to do. Allen is tired of doing without and wants to spend his money on things that he can enjoy now.

Eventually, Kathleen's need for control over their finances spilled over into other areas of their relationship. "I have no freedom," explained Allen. "I want to spend more time with my friends, work on my car, or just be by myself, but Kathleen wants to do everything together all the time."

One day, Allen had finally had enough. While Kathleen was out of town, he moved into his own apartment. Kathleen was furious because he was wasting money on rent when they owned a perfectly good four-bedroom house. "She's just worried about the money," sighed Allen. "She's totally missing the point."

Allen and Kathleen are both trying to establish their own behavior pattern as the foundation for their relationship, and it's clearly not working. Kathleen's concerns about money trace back to her memories of begging her father for money to spend on fun activities. Those memories inspired her to save as much as possible so that she could enjoy fun activities in her retirement. In the process, however, Kathleen ended up denying Allen's requests to spend money, the same way that her father had denied her.

Allen also comes from a rigid family where he felt compelled to rescue his mother from his domineering father. His battle with Kathleen over control of financial decisions traces back to a rebellion against the rigid rules of his parents' relationship. In the process, he accumulated a large debt, which placed even more stress on his marriage.

It took more than a year for Allen and Kathleen to learn how to communicate with each other. They both felt neglected, and their rigid families had left them ill-equipped to share their wants and needs with each other. Eventually, they were able to understand each other's positions and work toward reconciliation. They still disagree about financial issues on occasion, but money is no longer the center of a power struggle.

Taking Care of Business

In order to resolve your power struggles, you need to be willing to come together, communicate your feelings, and negotiate your differences. The goal is to attain a balance of power between you in an atmosphere of trust where you can both express your individuality and be acknowledged and appreciated for your contributions to the relationship. Let's take a closer look at the five developmental tasks that couples face in the power struggle stage.

1. Redefine Power

What does power have to do with marriage? In a word—everything. Rollo May describes power as a "fundamental aspect of the life process."[1]

When I ask couples to list words associated with power, the usual responses include control, authority, strength, influence, dominance, violence, and aggression. These words all pertain to exerting power for the purpose of domination.

We also see power play out in the competitive nature of our society where the win-lose attitude spills over into relationships. Like Allen and Kathleen, many people come from families with one dominant and one submissive parent. These families put a great deal of emphasis on doing things right. "It's my way or the highway," and any opposing viewpoint is wrong. This either/or world view leaves no room for considering other people's contributions as valid, appropriate, or worthy of consideration. Over time, it creates a culture of blamers and the blamed, or of victimizers and victims.

Another definition of power, however, is the "ability to act or produce an effect."[2] The Latin word for power (*posse*) means "to be able." In terms of marriage, this definition means that both of you have the ability or capacity to do something in order to complete tasks and achieve goals. Establishing and maintaining a satisfactory relationship with respect to power includes:

- Establishing a joint decision-making process

- Sharing responsibilities such as managing finances, household tasks, and parenting

- Creating the structure that enables you to complete these day-to-day activities

- Developing boundaries that are flexible enough to permit testing and experimentation with the roles of the relationship

- Learning how to compromise in order to work through differences

Power within the context of a marriage relationship also includes self-realization and self-actualization. In this view, power permits you to confront your conflicts in a more effective way. The exertion of dominating power always results in conflict, and many people view conflict as something to avoid at all cost. In most cases, our family experiences with conflict involve yelling and screaming, fighting, or verbal and physical abuse. Other families tend to respond with silence, withdrawal, or compliance to uphold peace at any price. In both violent and silent families, when we avoid conflict, we sacrifice our true selves.

It is better to view conflict as an opportunity for learning and growth. Because you and your partner are unique, you can agree to view your differences and differentness as enhancing your relationship rather than as a threat or grounds for rejection. This enables you to complete the remaining tasks of the power struggle stage:

- Resolving unfinished business within the family of origin
- Expanding the boundaries of marriage to include your vulnerabilities
- Appreciating and accepting your differences
- Laying a more empathetic foundation for an intimate relationship

2. Resolve Unfinished Business

People are pretty good at solving problems that relate to the present. It's the problems fueled by unconscious issues from the past that really pack a punch. It takes time, effort, and energy to uncover the real issues behind these problems.

When an argument is intense, repetitive, and continues over an extended period of time, it is almost always rooted in unfinished business from the past. When these issues are not resolved, couples fall into argument ruts, replaying the same arguments over and over again without ever getting to the heart of the conflict.

If you're stuck in an argument rut, try writing an argument script. Write out your version of the argument, and compare notes with your partner. Through this exercise, you should begin to see the repetition. Then ask yourself the following questions:

- What is it about the situation that upsets me? Don't think about the situation itself (for example, an argument over an unmade bed). Instead, think about why it's an issue at all. (When my partner doesn't make the bed, it makes me feel like he/she doesn't love me enough to respond to a simple request.)

_____

_____

_____

_____

- What is the emotion behind this argument? Am I hurt, angry, frustrated, jealous, overwhelmed, disappointed, etc.?

_____

_____

_____

_____

- At what other times in my life have I experienced this same emotion (with friends, family, etc.)? Who was involved in the situation, and how was it resolved?

_____

_____

_____

_____

The purpose of this exercise is not to place the blame on your family but rather to discover how family interactions from the past might be influencing the behaviors demonstrated in your present relationship. It is only by recogniz- ing these patterns of past behavior that you can take responsibility for your own thoughts, feelings, and actions in the present and begin the process of change.

The process of separating present problems from past wounds requires time, patience, and empathy from both partners. It may also require that you expand the boundaries of your relationship to accept new communication and behavioral patterns.

3. Expand the Boundaries of the Relationship

Are you sensing a theme? When it comes to relationships, the boundaries and blueprints are never set in stone. The nature of your relationship will continue to evolve as you and your partner explore new aspects of your individuality and your life together.

In the honeymoon stage, couples develop the boundaries that define the parameters of their couple relationship. In the expectation stage, they expand those boundaries to let each partner express his or her own views and opinions. In the power struggle stage, the boundaries must expand once again as both partners reveal hidden aspects of their selves. There must be room for both you and your partner in the relationship, and that means accepting your partner for who that person really is, not for who you want him or her to be.

Power struggles that simmer under the surface for years often erupt during times of change such as the birth of a child, a move, a job transition, or any other point where uncertainty challenges the status quo. As Ashley and Matt discover in the following vignette, sometimes the boundaries that worked for you in the past no longer cover the complexities of a new situation.

> *Ashley and Matt had been married for four years before they had their first child. During that time, they had dealt with a number of conflicts that pertained to their marriage, but with the arrival of their son Andrew, they found themselves engaged in a power struggle.*
>
> *"Matt just doesn't understand how to be a good father," said Ashley. "I leave specific instructions about how to care for the baby, but he doesn't follow them."*

Matt slumps against the back of the chair, visibly discouraged by Ashley's comments. "I take care of Andrew three evenings a week while Ashley works," explains Matt, "and I think that I do a good job of caring for Andrew and doing the chores that she leaves for me." Ashley is quick to point out that she often has to redo a lot of the tasks that Matt completes because he doesn't do them right.

By the time they arrived in my office, Matt was ready to give up. "I want to be a part of my son's life and a part of this marriage, but nothing that I do is ever good enough for Ashley. Why does she ask for my help when it's obvious that she thinks I'm an idiot?"

Through our discussions, Ashley realized that her issue with Matt wasn't about his parenting skills at all. When Ashley started kindergarten, her mother took on a full-time job and had less time to spend with Ashley and her sister. Although Matt and Ashley had agreed that Ashley would continue working after Andrew was born, now that the situation was upon her, she remembered how she felt when her mom returned to work and felt guilty about leaving Andrew. When she realized the real motivation behind her controlling behavior, Ashley was able to recognize that Matt was very capable and that she could trust him to follow through on tasks, even if he didn't do them the way that she would prefer.

When Matt understood that Ashley's behavior wasn't connected to her opinion of him, he was more willing to communicate his own desires and opinions on how they could better share parenting responsibilities and household tasks. By understanding each other's backgrounds, they were better able to see the true source of their conflict.

In this case, their power struggle over Andrew led Ashley and Matt to reevaluate their roles in the relationship. Ashley had to expand her boundaries to include Matt as an equal partner in the parenting process. Matt had to expand his boundaries to accept Ashley's past experiences and work with her to establish a healthy balance between work and parenting in their marriage. Matt also had to learn how to take a more proactive role in making decisions about the baby, and Ashley had to learn how to view his opinions and ideas as a valuable contribution to their relationship.

While it may only take a few minutes to realize the root of the problem, it can take years to actually resolve these conflicts. The key is to start resolving conflicts and changing communication processes as soon as the problems become apparent, and not when they have escalated into full-blown power struggles.

4. Accept the Strengths and the Limitations

Accepting your partner's strengths and limitations is an important step toward reconciling the differences that lead to power struggles. In fact, accepting both the ups and the downs of a relationship is so foundational to a healthy marriage that the concept is written right into the vows.

> *I, (bride/groom), take you, (groom/bride), to be my (wife/husband), to have and to hold from this day forward, for better or for worse, for richer or for poorer, in sickness and in health, to love and to cherish; from this day forward until death do us part.*

It is easy to accept the characteristics that lead to better, richer, and health. It is the worse, poorer, and sickness traits that tend to escalate the power struggles. As you work through your unfinished business from the past, some of the reasons behind these characteristics should surface, making it easier for both of you to understand the motivation behind the behavior.

There is a story told about a husband and wife who were celebrating their fiftieth wedding anniversary. Having spent most of the day with family and friends at a big party given in their honor, they decided to have a snack before heading to bed. They went into the kitchen, where the husband opened up a new loaf of bread and handed the end piece to his wife. She exploded. She said, "For fifty years you have been dumping the heel of the bread on me. I will not take it anymore, this lack of concern for me and what I like." On and on she went, berating her husband for giving her the heel of the bread. The husband was absolutely astonished at her outburst. When she had finished, he said to her quietly, "But it's my favorite piece."[3]

It is so easy to jump to conclusions based on our own frame of reference. In this case, what the husband intended to be a gesture of love and self-sacrifice, his wife interpreted as inconsideration. Oftentimes, when we understand the motivation behind a behavior, we have a much easier time accepting it.

Using the guidelines below, spend a few moments honestly reflecting on your own strengths and limitations. Where do they come from (description/ background)? Why do you think you practice them (motivation)? Then, without being judgmental, take a few minutes to jot down some of your partner's strengths and limitations using the same strategy.

Who am I?	Description/Background	Motivation
I am encouraging (positive).	I like helping people. I had a teacher who really encouraged me to succeed, and it motivated me.	• Connecting with people • Affirmation of my own worth • Seeing other people happy makes me happy.
I am a perfectionist (negative).	My mom was a perfectionist, and I liked living in an orderly environment. I've always been very successful in life, and I don't think that people can do things as well as I can. I never liked group projects and often would rather do something myself than have someone else do it a way that I don't like.	• Affirmation and recognition from other people • Wanting to make a good impression • Hiding shyness with accomplishments

A character inventory in black and white can be overwhelming and even a bit discouraging at first. Exposing weaknesses increases vulnerability, and no one wants to parade his or her faults before the world. But taking a good look at reality is a prerequisite to change. And ultimately, the only person in a power struggle that you can change is yourself. You can change how you act and react toward your partner's strengths and limitations. Assuming that neither of those characteristics is life threatening, choose to accept them both.

*   *   *

Marriage Tool #3: Conflict Resolution

One of the most powerful things that you can do for your marriage is to learn how you and your partner can constructively handle your differences and disagreements.

Through his twenty-year study of two thousand couples, John Gottman determined that the key to marital happiness "results from a couple's ability to resolve the conflicts that are inevitable in any relationships."[4] The idea that happy couples never fight is utterly false. They do fight, but they fight fairly because they understand each other's strengths and weaknesses.

When conflict stirs up intense emotions, it is important to take a time out from the issue at hand to determine if the emotions come from the actual conflict or if they are connected to an experience from the past. Many times, couples believe they are arguing over one thing (a wife's failure to put dirty dishes in the dishwasher, for example) when the conflict is really about something else (the husband feeling as if his wife doesn't acknowledge his requests). If you do not discover the true root of these emotions, you will continue to argue in circles.

Try following these steps to practice conflict resolution:

- **Pick a designated time and a neutral location for the discussion.**

  This allows you to approach the conflict in a less confrontational state of mind. Pick a neutral location for your discussions, and never use the bedroom. Save that room for its intended purposes.

- **Use common courtesy.**

  Fight fairly. Don't attack your partner's weaknesses to gain the upper hand.

- **Set discussion goals, and stick to the topic.**

  Discuss the root of the problem, not just the symptoms. Limit the discussion to approximately thirty minutes to avoid emotional marathons.

- **Start with neutral facts.**

  Without placing blame, describe how each of you contributes to the conflict.

- **State your opinions and feelings.**

  Explain how the event made you feel, and, if possible, why it made you feel that way.

- **Prepare to negotiate.**

  Discuss possible ways to resolve the conflict, including unsuccessful attempts to resolve this issue in the past.

- **Chart a course.**

  Pick the solution that best meets the needs of both partners. You may not get everything you want, but you should both get what you need.

- **Review the outcome.**

Set a time to review the resolution in the future. Has the conflict truly been resolved, or is it popping up in other places? If you're not satisfied with the outcome, don't be afraid to try a different solution.

- **Celebrate your success.**

  When the problem truly is resolved, reward each other. Find a way to commemorate and celebrate that accomplishment.

*   *   *

5. Lay a Foundation of Empathy and Connectedness

Empathy is a key ingredient to resolving a power struggle. When you know how to empathize with each other, you can stay focused on and connected in the present. Responding to each other's pain with empathy and understanding is vital for increasing the intimate bond between you.

There are no cookie-cutter people. Everyone is an original, and each person has his or her own perception of reality based on past experiences. The key to building empathy is to understand your partner's perceptions and point of view. In the 1950s, Joseph Luft and Harry Ingram introduced the Johari Window[5] as a tool to illustrate this type of awareness in relationships.

The Johari Window	Known to Self	Not Known to Self
Known to Others	**I** Area of Free Activity: Things that we know and that others know about us	**II** Blind Area: Things that others can see in us, but that do not see in ourselves
Not Known to Others	**III** Avoided or Hidden Area: Things that we know about ourselves, but do not reveal to others	**IV** Area of Unknown Activity: Things we don't know and that others aren't aware of, that influence our relationships

In the early stages of a relationship, Quadrant I is very small. However, as you get to know each other, Quadrant I increases in size and Quadrant III tends to decrease. As you grow closer, you feel more comfortable being yourselves and perceiving others as they really are. In an environment of mutual love and trust, it becomes less necessary to hide your true thoughts and feelings.

Quadrants II and IV usually take longer to change size because we often have good reasons, or at least good excuses, for blinding ourselves from some of the things that we think, feel, or do. As you and your partner evaluate your past experiences and are able to share your motivations and perceptions with each other, these quadrants slowly decrease and true empathy begins to grow.

Take a few moments to answer the following questions to see how you measure up in the empathy department:

1. Do you feel safe (emotionally, spiritually, physically) when you express your innermost thoughts and feelings to your partner? Why or why not?

    _____

    _____

    _____

    _____

2. When you feel vulnerable, do you ask for emotional support from your partner? Why or why not?

    _____

    _____

    _____

    _____

3. How do you ask for the emotional support that you need?

    _____

    _____

    _____

4. Do you expect to get that support when you ask?

_____

_____

_____

_____

5. Would your partner say that you are emotionally responsive to his/her vulnerability?

_____

_____

_____

_____

6. Do you take an active role in nourishing your relationship? Does your partner do the same? How?

_____

_____

_____

_____

When you are ready, share your answers with your partner to begin building a more empathetic relationship.

Getting Stuck

Couples get stuck in a power struggle when they are unable to break the cycle of accusation and blame—when they simply cannot let go of their own positions, perceptions, and points of view. These partners ultimately follow one of two paths: ① they become violent, lashing out at each other in their attempts to gain control; or ② they become silent, creating great distance between them as a shield against continued pain and anguish. Violence in this stage almost always results in serious injury. Silence creates an emotional divorce, in which the two begin to live separate lives in the same physical space.

Although you might believe that calling it quits will resolve a power struggle, those who divorce during this stage almost always end up fighting about something else (children, property, money, etc.) through their lawyers, the courts, and custody battles.

Unresolved power struggles can last for weeks, months, and even years. If the intensity of the situation reaches a point at which neither you nor your partner is able to work toward resolution, it's definitely time to seek some outside help.

Do Try This at Home: Conflict Resolution

The point of this exercise is to connect your current conflict in the present with its root from the past and to determine where the pain originated. In many cases, your power struggle mirrors a conflict from your parents' marriages or from your own childhood experiences. If these conflicts are not resolved, they will continue to dominate every aspect of the relationship.

Take some time away from your partner to answer the questions below regarding a specific power-struggle issue. Then set aside some time to come together as a couple to discuss your answers.

1. What do I want to get out of this situation?

_____

_____

_____

_____

2. What (if anything) am I contributing to the problem?

_____

_____

_____

_____

3. Does the current problem connect to an experience in my past?

_____

_____

_____

4. What incident in the present initiated the current problem?

_____

_____

_____

5. What will happen if I take my partner's point of view?

_____

_____

_____

6. What will happen if I try to take control of the situation?

_____

_____

_____

7. What is the best resolution for everyone involved?

_____

_____

_____

_____

8. How can I prevent this from happening in the future?

_____

_____

_____

_____

As you share your answers with your partner, be open to listening, hearing, and sharing points of view. If the tension and stress escalate, stop the discussion and spend twenty to thirty minutes (or even twenty-four hours) apart to calm down and refocus on the real issues.

Moving On

The power struggle is the most difficult, distressing, and divisive stage in a marriage, but if you do not get past it, you will not be prepared to deal with the separation and individuation process that repeats itself in the seven-year-itch stage.

Recognizing and relinquishing the need to be in control is the first step toward transitioning out of the power struggle. As you take small steps to reconnect and choose cooperation and intimacy over domination, you will be better able to understand and acknowledge your partner's contributions as valid, appropriate, and worthy of consideration. As Rilke says,

> Once the realization is accepted that even between the closest human beings infinite distances continue to exist, a wonderful living side by side can grow up, if they succeed in loving the distance between them

which makes it possible for each to see each other whole against the sky.[6]

Although it may not seem possible in the midst of the battle, there can be life, even joy, after a power struggle. As you begin to understand each other's pain and work to change your own behavior, you can develop the conflict-resolution skills and empathy necessary to enjoy a satisfying and fulfilling relationship.

Stage Four: The Seven-Year Itch

Let there be spaces in your togetherness
And let the winds of heaven dance between you.
... and stand together, yet not too near together.
For the pillars of the temple stand apart
And the oak tree and the cypress grow not
in each other's shadow.
~ Kahlil Gibran[1]
(*The Prophet*)

I like to call the fourth stage of marriage the "seven-year itch." This is a period when one or both partners become restless within the relationship. They are dissatisfied with the status quo and begin to develop "wanderlust," as one of my clients so aptly described it.

The seven-year itch revolves around unfinished separation-individuation issues related to dependence and independence from each partner's past and frequently occurs in the middle years of marriage. Earlier in the marriage, couples are consumed by the expectation and power-struggle stages and often miss the first seven-year itch. Usually by the fourteenth or fifteenth year, however, their children are approaching adolescence, and as their children deal with the struggles of growing up and creating independent identities, their parents often find themselves reliving their own struggles.

Even couples without children deal with increasing change and tension in the middle years of marriage. Age brings with it a growing desire to resolve unfinished business and inspires many adults to ask questions about their own childhoods or to rebuild relationships with their parents.

The struggle for independence marks a major change in the marriage journey. Some people become adamant about getting a job, returning to school, or traveling more now that the children are older. Others might pursue new relationships, which often lead to affairs.

I remember treating one couple who retired in their sixties. One day, the husband came home and said to his wife, "Well, the children are all grown and out of the house. We've remodeled the house the way that you wanted it. Now it's my turn to do my thing." Then he packed his bags and left. This "It's my turn—I want to do something for myself" attitude permeates the seven-year-itch stage as each partner begins to think, "I can make myself happy. I can take care of myself. I need some time or space for myself."

A general sense of frustration seeps into the relationship as both partners recognize the validity of their own needs but are frustrated by the timing of those needs. It's as if one or both partners have been operating on autopilot for years and then suddenly wake up and ask, "Who am I? How did I lose my identity in this relationship?" This is especially true of women who devote their early married years to motherhood. When the children are older and require less hands-on attention, these women struggle to find their place in the family. The same is true of highly educated people who spend most of their youth pursuing academic and career-focused goals. When they achieve those goals (of becoming doctors, lawyers, etc.), they wake up one day, realize that they missed their adolescence, and feel a desperate need to make up for lost time or relive experiences that they didn't fully appreciate the first time around.

The physical and emotional distance between partners in this stage seems immeasurable. Threats of separation and divorce increase, usually as attempts to force the more independent partner back into the old relationship patterns. There can be a great deal of back-and-forth movement; couples may separate for short periods of time and then move back in together. One or both partners feel a strong need "to find themselves," and yet the pull to be together is still very powerful. There is a constant conflict over the need to support each other's growth and independence and yet still pursue an intimate relationship. When the partners do return to the relationship, however, they often fall back into their old patterns, increasing their frustration.

Real Life: Keith and Audrey

Keith and Audrey have been in and out of counseling for six of the twelve years that they have been married. In the first session of this round, Audrey got right to the point.

"Keith never takes any responsibility with the kids or the house, and I'm tired of always being the grown-up in this marriage," she said. "When we first got married, I didn't mind as much because he was logging a ton of flight hours to get a job with a commercial airline, and Erin was my daughter from a previous relationship so I didn't expect him to jump into parenting right away. But now that he's got a good job with a consistent schedule, I expect more. We have two more children of our own

now, and I'm always picking up the slack. I'm exhausted and completely miserable."

About two weeks ago, Keith was so fed up with Audrey's expectations that he moved out. "I just wanted a break from the constant pressure to live up to Audrey's standards," explained Keith. "I have a stressful job that takes me away from home for three or four days at a time, and when I get back, I just want to unwind and have some fun. But she wants me to fix things around the house, go to events with her friends that I don't even know, or babysit the kids so that she can go out."

Taking Care of Business

Most people going through a seven-year (or fourteen-year or twenty-one-year or twenty-eight-year) itch don't even recognize this as a new stage within the relationship. They assume that they've hit another rough patch, or even a brick wall, and that there is no point in moving forward. However, if you can weather this storm and complete the required developmental tasks, you will be well positioned for a lifetime of love and intimacy. Let's take a closer look at the three developmental tasks that couples face in the seven-year-itch stage.

1. Achieve Independence within the Relationship

The early years of marriage can encompass a lot of change. You move in together and merge two households, one or both of you are pursuing an education or a career, and oftentimes children join the family—all within the first five to seven years of the marriage relationship. In the midst of all of this change, it's easy to feel as though your real identity has been lost in the shuffle. Now is the time for you and your partner to take a good, long look in the mirror and decide if what you are doing now is what you want to do for the rest of your lives.

Please don't misunderstand this point; I am not suggesting that you walk away from your marriage. Many people mistakenly believe that the best way to find themselves is to leave their current relationships and start fresh with someone else. This rarely works; unless you deal with the unresolved issues in your current relationship (most of which stem from unfinished business from the past), you will carry those issues into your next relationship. What I am asking you to do is to make sure that you and your partner are continuing to grow as separate individuals as well as in your relationship together. In the case of Keith and Audrey, their personal growth had hit a brick wall.

Audrey, who had planned to be an architect, got pregnant with Erin in her freshman year of college. Although she had tried to finish her degree, the demands of motherhood dashed her career goals, and she took a retail job to pay the bills. "When I met Keith, I fell in love with his focus and drive," said Audrey. "He reminded me of my life before Erin, and I wanted to be around that kind of passion." Over time, however, Audrey began to resent Keith's career because early parenthood had limited her opportunity to have one of her own.

Now that Erin has just earned her driver's license, Audrey is also terrified that she'll make the same mistakes that Audrey did. While wanting to protect Erin, she's also jealous of her freedom. "I never really had a chance to run around and have fun," explained Audrey. "I was a mom, so I started spending time with other moms. I feel like I missed something." By putting her education, her career, and essentially her young adulthood on hold, Audrey felt trapped in her current situation.

For Keith, it was a case of professional burnout. "I've always been interested in airplanes, but now that I think about it, I don't remember really wanting to be a pilot," said Keith in a one-on-one session. "My dad was in the Air Force, and we liked to talk about planes, so when I had to choose a career path, it seemed like a natural fit." Ten years down the road, however, Keith feels trapped in a job that puts a lot of stress on his marriage. "I can't come home every night like other husbands, so most of the day-to-day stuff falls to Audrey," he explained. "She's really good at it, but it's like being the perfect parent has become her mission in life, and I just don't need that kind of pressure. I have enough to deal with in the air when lives depend on me. This other stuff—picking up clothes, going to birthday parties—it just isn't that serious to me."

It turns out that Keith's dad had a similar attitude. As a fighter pilot, he was gone for months at a time, leaving Keith's mom to run the household. Without a day-to-day model of fatherhood, Keith was ill equipped to be a father to Audrey's daughter Erin or to their own children later on.

When personal growth comes to a halt, relationship growth suffers as well. In situations like this, both partners need to be flexible enough to let the other try new things and to resolve any remaining unfinished business from the past.

Unfortunately, there is no simple solution for accomplishing this task. Each person must go about it in his or her own way.

- Will one of you return to work, stop working, or change career fields?
- Will one of you go back to school to complete a degree or pursue continuing education?
- Will you have more children?
- Will you move to a different home or even a different city or state?
- Will you reestablish relationships with friends and family members that may have been lost during the early years of marriage?
- Will you pursue dreams and desires that were too expensive or time-consuming during your early parenting years?

These types of questions are very important to consider, and as a couple you will need to negotiate the boundaries and roles of your relationship to absorb this period of independence and exploration.

Staying connected to your partner as you pursue your independence is absolutely critical. If you do not continue to build your relationship together while you are working through your individual issues of independence, your marriage will suffer. Continue to spend twenty minutes a day talking. Keep dating each other on a weekly basis, and remember to enjoy a night away together now and then.

2. Strengthen Your Negotiation Skills

Henry Boyle once said, "The most important trip you may take in life is meeting people half way." In marriage, the art of negotiation is one of the most important skills you'll ever learn. It is particularly important during this stage of increased independence as you and your partner negotiate new roles and expectations for your relationship.

It takes a great deal of trust to negotiate needs and wants within a relationship. To be able to say "I want" takes courage. Many people are reluctant to ask for something for themselves for fear of sounding selfish, while others make demands, expecting every wish to be fulfilled. Still others grow angry, resentful, and defiant when they don't get what they want—whether they have asked for it or not.

Both Keith and Audrey wanted to make changes in their lives, but neither knew how to introduce that idea into the relationship. Audrey wanted to return to school to finish her degree, but she couldn't see how to make that work with Keith's schedule. Keith wanted to transition into a job with more regular hours, but he was afraid that being home more would mean answering to Audrey about everything. Neither of them grew up in families that left much room for negotiation. As a result, neither of them knew how to ask for what they want or need.

*   *   *

Marriage Tool #4: Negotiation

Negotiation is similar to both problem solving and conflict resolution in process, but it requires more commitment from each side. There are five basic elements to a successful negotiation:

- **Express your commitment to the relationship.**

  People are afraid to be honest about their needs and wants when they feel threatened. By affirming your loyalty to the marriage, you are creating a safe environment in which to work through difficult issues without the fear of abandonment.

- **Clearly state the need or want.**

  "Clearly" is the key. Many negotiations are ground to a halt by faulty communication. Know what you want, and be prepared to explain it in more than one way if necessary.

- **Respond to the need or want.**

  Listening to each other is very important. While your partner lays out his or her position, listen attentively and acknowledge the need or want, whether you agree with it or not.

- **Seek a mutually acceptable solution.**

  If you both understand and accept the expressed need or want, determine what each of you will need to do to reach that goal. If one of you rejects the other's need or want, then you need to work together to find a solution that satisfies both of you.

- **Decide who will do what and when.**

  You and your partner need to outline what you are and are not willing to do and listen to each other's plans. Come up with a timetable so that you will know when the task is finished. It is very important to complete this step without resorting to bargaining, coercion, threats, or punishment.

The best outcome to any negotiation may not even be the solution but rather the confidence that comes from realizing that situations and people can change. As you begin to see problems resolved and gradual improvement in the relationship, this will increase your desire to spend time with your partner, which can eventually infuse your marriage with a new level of energy and excitement.

In his business-focused books, Max Bazerman[2] cites five common pitfalls to the art of negotiation. The same principles can just as easily be applied to the negotiations between spouses.

- You believe that your partner must lose in order for you to win.

  Negotiation is not a competitive sport. There are no winners or losers in a negotiation because each party walks away with a resolution that meets his or her needs, even if it doesn't give them everything that they want.

- You plunge ahead without all of the appropriate information.

  Make sure that you know what you're talking about. Don't just rely on feelings or memories; get the facts.

- You make extreme demands.

  If you make extreme demands that you cannot support, it becomes virtually impossible to back down. Even if your partner does cave in to those demands, you would be hard-pressed to put them into action. As a warning sign, watch for circumstances in which you use anger to force your partner into agreement.

- You ignore an unbiased outside opinion.

  While your position might seem completely fair and rational to you, you might be surprised at how many other people would disagree. There is nothing wrong with bringing in a neutral third party (a pastor, counselor, etc.) to evaluate the fairness of your proposed solution.

- You think only of what you will lose.

  While most people will take a certain small gain over a risky greater gain, they won't accept a certain small loss over a possible larger loss. Resist the urge to cut your losses completely. Rather, accept a small personal loss for the greater good of your marriage. As French writer Joseph Joubert so perfectly phrased it, "Never cut what you can untie."

*   *   *

3. Choose the Relationship

Although you have already been married for a number of years, this stage requires both you and your partner to consciously choose your relationship as a way of life. Falling in love is an unconscious choice, and when you got married you didn't know each other nearly as well as you do now.

I recommend that both partners spend some time dreaming about the future of their marriage by asking the following questions[3]:

> **What is the purpose of my relationship with my partner?**
> Have you ever really thought about the reason for your relationship? Is it to provide you with love and support? Is it for security? Is it to bring children into the world? Is it to have companionship? Once you know your reason for being, it's much easier to set priorities within and for the relationship.
>
> **What goals do I have for improving this relationship over the next (one/five/ten) years?**
> Think about your relationship from both short-term and long-term perspectives. What do you want to accomplish? Where do you want to end up? Now is the time to begin positioning yourself in that direction as a couple. To do this, you will need to share a common vision and make decisions together.
>
> **What goals do I have for improving myself over the next (one/five/ten) years?**
> This question corresponds nicely with the first developmental task of achieving independence within the relationship. As you answer this question, however, think about your answers in the context of your goals for the relationship. How do they line up? Can you and your partner find a way to accommodate both? If you only focus on your own development and dreams during this stage, the marriage will fall apart because the two of you will inevitably move in different directions. The point of this choice is to let both you and your partner be yourselves, and to still be married.

Take some time to compare notes with your partner. Are you working toward the same goals, or are you creating conflict by moving in opposite directions?

As you contemplate the changes that you want to make now—leaving the marriage, changing jobs, moving to a new house, returning to school, traveling—ask yourself how they fit within the big picture of the relationship. If the current actions help you meet your relationship goals, go forward. If they don't, work toward a better solution that will help you both move forward.

For Keith and Audrey, individual and couples therapy helped them answer these questions. They decided that Audrey would return to school to finish her degree. Over the years, she had buried her resentment toward Keith and jealousy of Erin's freedom into her parenting and homemaking responsibilities. When she was able to return to the field that she loved, she was more comfortable at home and less likely to leave the children with Keith in order to escape.

Keith eventually found a corporate position with a major aircraft manufacturer in another state. Although it meant moving across country, Audrey was willing to compromise because the new job gave Keith more time at home. With Audrey in class two nights a week, she had to let go of her control over the household and let Keith take over some of the parenting responsibilities. Although Audrey still has high standards for their relationship, they are now driven by a desire to work on the marriage and not by her feelings of inadequacy or loss. With less pressure at work and at home, Keith is more engaged in his relationship with Audrey and more willing to pitch in with the kids.

"I wanted to leave the marriage because I had no idea how to make this work," said Keith. "I was so miserable, but I just assumed that Audrey was the problem. I wasn't even looking at my own issues. Our life isn't perfect now, but it works."

Getting Stuck

People who did not completely separate from their parents as adolescents, people who were abused as children, and people pulled into adolescent behavior by their own children's teenage years tend to get stuck in this stage.

For everyone else, the choice is less complex: you choose the relationship, seek help in restoring it, and move on, or you choose to leave. Either way, this choice should be made with the help of a professional counselor or therapist.

The Structured Trial Separation

With my clients, I use a trial separation period that provides the couple with time apart to get a clearer perspective of the relationship as well as with an opportunity to develop a sense of self. From this vantage point, they are then able to make a clear decision about their choice to leave or stay in the relationship. Working through this process with a therapist reduces the impulse for one partner to pack up and leave with little explanation. Structured trial separations work well when: (1) the couple wants to save the marriage; (2) the level of anger and conflict in the relationship has escalated to a point where neither partner can reach an objective position; (3) an affair has been discovered or revealed; or (4) one partner repeatedly leaves the relationship and returns, only to fall into old patterns of behavior.

The purpose of a trial separation is to prevent further damage to the relationship by providing enough space for the partners to gain more realistic perspectives and realize that they do miss each other and want to spend time together. There is always a risk that one partner might decide not to return, but we discuss that risk up front, and each partner is encouraged to express his or her fears and concerns about this possibility. Of the hundreds of couples that I have worked with over the years, on average only one couple a year chooses divorce over restoring their relationship.

A trial separation also gives each person time to focus on his or her own wants and needs and to separate them from the needs of the relationship. As one client explained it, "I didn't realize that I had a need to be alone and follow my own interests until we separated. Now, I know how to ask for what I want." The time apart gives each person an opportunity to realize that he or she can be a self-reliant individual.

This period of time is also an opportunity for the partners to evaluate their own dysfunctional repetitive patterns in the relationship. By doing this apart from the spouse, they are able to take responsibility for their own behaviors rather than blaming them on the partner.

Ground Rules

In order to set up a trial separation, the couple sees a therapist to review the purpose of the separation and to establish the ground rules that both partners will follow. These guidelines must be flexible enough to meet the needs of both people. We discuss the following topics thoroughly:

- Therapy

- Who will move
- Family finances
- Length of separation
- Childcare (if children are involved)
- Contact and dating
- Returning to the relationship

Therapy: For the trial separation to serve its intended purpose, both partners must have a safe place where they can express themselves and practice their communication skills. I recommend individual therapy for each spouse on alternate weeks and couples therapy on the third week. That way, each person has time to focus on individual issues, and then they come together to work through their insights and practice their new interpersonal skills. Ideally, the couple should work with the same therapist, as couples seeing different therapists tend to be pulled in different directions.

Who Will Move: This is the first decision in any separation. Sometimes it's an easy decision because one partner is already intent on leaving. In other cases, it may take several weeks to iron out the details. Some people attempt to divide their household into two separate living arrangements. This is rarely successful. Moving in with friends or family members is also not a good choice because this situation usually defeats the purpose of being alone to gain perspective on the relationship and explore personal issues.

Family Finances: Maintaining two households is expensive. The couple must agree on how to support each other and the family financially during the separation.

Length of Separation: An effective trial separation usually spans a minimum of three months. This is the minimum amount of time needed for couples to transition into single life and single parenthood. This is also enough time for the partners to realize that they do miss each other and to realistically understand the work that needs to be done to restore the relationship. Some couples choose to extend this period to six or twelve months in order to work through the pain and anger connected with the marriage (particularly in the case of an affair), to deal with dysfunctional communication patterns, or to resolve extensive unfinished business from the past.

Childcare: Not only must the partners work out an agreeable parenting schedule, but they must also explain to their children why they are choosing to separate. Children fear divorce, and it is difficult for them to understand how time apart is a positive step in avoiding divorce. The more conflict there is between the parents, the more disruptive the separation will be for the children. Family therapy can be helpful during these times to give the children an opportunity to express their own fears and feelings.

Contact and Dating: Personal contact between the partners requires careful negotiation. Early on, I discourage frequent phone calls and dropping in on each other. Other than therapy, the couple should avoid contact with each other for the first month. When they do see each other again, it should be in a neutral setting (a restaurant, a park, etc.) and not in their places of residence.

As time passes, the couple can explore dating experiences again. I encourage both partners to call the other to make a conscious effort to plan fun activities together. By this point in their marriage, many couples forget how to have fun together. I encourage both partners to develop a list of things that they would like to do or try and then invite their partner to join them.

The couple must also negotiate the issue of dating other people. Affairs during this period are counterproductive and distract people from the purpose of the separation. Each couple must agree, with the guidance of their therapist, to the level of interaction with the opposite sex that is appropriate during the separation.

Reestablishing the couple's sexual relationship is also discussed in therapy. This is especially important if either person has had problems asking for the kind of sexual activity that they desire or if one partner has had an affair.

Returning to the Relationship: An important transition occurs when one partner wants to return to the relationship. When both partners are comfortable with this arrangement, their therapist helps them negotiate the details of this process as well.

By this time, the partners are usually more confident about themselves as individuals, and they know how they want to relate to each other as a couple. They have put considerable time, money, and energy into redesigning their relationship, developing communication skills, and negotiating their needs and desires. They have achieved a renewed sense of love and respect for each other's unique characteristics and enjoy a newly found ability to openly discuss the issues that come between them. They feel comfortable pursuing independent interests and activities and also enjoy each other when they are together.

Do Try This at Home: Separateness and Togetherness

Take some time away from your partner to answer the following questions. Then set aside some time to come together as a couple to discuss your answers.

1. Do you support your partner's development as an individual? How? Give an example.

    _____

    _____

    _____

    _____

2. Do you support your partner's growth as an individual even when you don't agree? How? Give an example.

    _____

    _____

    _____

    _____

3. Do you believe that your partner is giving at least 50 percent to the relationship? Is that enough? Would you like more or less?

    _____

    _____

    _____

    _____

4. Do you and your partner share any joint commitments to projects, work, activities, or social causes? If so, what?

    _____

_____

_____

_____

5. Did you deliberately decide to create something together in one of
    those areas? Why or why not?

_____

_____

_____

_____

6. Does this project seem to add or detract from the bond between you?
    How?

_____

_____

_____

_____

The answers to these questions should spark a healthy debate as to the level
of separateness and togetherness that each of you feels within your relationship. If you are unhappy with the present situation, use these answers as a starting point to negotiate a new future.

As you share your answers with your partner, be open to listening, hearing,
and sharing points of view. If tension and stress escalate, stop the discussion
and spend twenty to thirty minutes (or even twenty-four hours) apart to calm
down and refocus on the real issues.

Moving On

A couple has successfully moved through the seven-year-itch stage when each
partner: is committed to the relationship, recognizes that he or she must resolve

his or her own issues, can state his or her needs and wants openly, and can maintain his or her own identity within the relationship.

As couples share the journey of exploring their own needs while still finding points of intersection and compromise, they are building a marriage of intimacy, love, and respect that will endure through any hardships to come.

Stage Five: Reconciliation ~ Viva la Difference!

What counts in making a happy marriage is not so much how compatible you are, but how you deal with incompatibility.
~ Leo Tolstoy

The last two stages of marriage, reconciliation and acceptance, are often the richest and most pleasurable. And so they should be. Couples who are willing to work through all of the hurts and hang-ups and grow together as individuals are fully prepared for the joy that comes from a mutually pleasurable and intimate relationship.

Although couples in these stages still experience some conflict, they know who they are and are secure enough in their relationships to confront their issues through open and honest negotiation. As a result, the relationship flows smoothly and naturally because both partners feel fully accepted and are fully accepting of each other. Their relationship is deeply rooted, giving both people the freedom to flourish.

Reconciliation

True reconciliation occurs when people realize that their partners are living, breathing, separate individuals who may never meet all of their expectations or fulfill all of their needs. *You have your issues and I have mine. I can't change you, you can't change me, and that's okay. I love you anyway!* Couples in this stage exhibit a greater ability to take responsibility for their own needs, ideas, thoughts, and feelings, and they accept the fact that those desires may be different from those of their partners'.

Reconciliation infuses relationships with a spirit of cooperation. Where one person once viewed his or her partner's personal growth and independence as rejection, he or she now experiences the joy and fulfillment that comes from embracing the partner's unique quirks and characteristics. They understand each other's strengths and limitations and work together to set boundaries, make decisions, and carry out daily activities.

The couples that I see in my practice usually reconcile their relationship after ten to fifteen years of marriage, sometimes even after twenty or more. The sad thing is that it doesn't have to take that long. There is no predetermined amount of time required to achieve a thriving relationship. The only factors influencing that timeline are you and your partner. Those who are willing to honestly evaluate themselves and their behavior are likely to reconcile early in their relationship. On the other end of the spectrum are those who, for whatever reason, are unwilling to explore even the possibility of growth. These couples often fall apart in earlier stages, too caught up in their own lives to truly embrace couplehood.

Real Life: Allen and Kathleen

You might remember Allen and Kathleen as the couple trapped in the power struggle over money. After spending several years working through their power struggle, they were able to reconcile their relationship.

> *Kathleen really struggled with reconciliation. Allen had been married once before and was now a grandfather. Although he was only distantly connected to his daughter, he wanted to help her out financially with the baby and continued to go into debt to do so. When Kathleen found out, she felt betrayed because they had agreed to a financial plan that Allen seemed to be ignoring. She felt as if he was putting more emphasis on his relationship with his estranged daughter than on her.*

> *As they continued to work through their issues about money, Allen shared his desire to reconnect with his daughter and how the money made him feel needed in that fatherly role. They ultimately agreed that Allen could continue to provide some financial support but that he should also reach out to rebuild the relationship as well. Through his reconciliation with Kathleen, Allen wrote letters to his daughter asking for her forgiveness and expressing a desire to reconnect with her when she was ready.*

By the time Allen and Kathleen finished their counseling sessions, they felt very good about what they had accomplished both as individuals and as a couple. Through exploring their families of origin, both learned that they knew nothing about being generous with money or with love. By realizing how ill equipped they had been, they were eventually able to forgive each other for the damage that they had each done to their relationship and work together to create the boundaries that best fit the unique aspects of their marriage.

Taking Care of Business

If you have completed many of the developmental tasks from the earlier stages, you are going to be in great shape at this point. And yet, there is no standing still in marriage. If you're not moving forward, you are spinning in circles, or you're actually moving backward—back into old habits and old ways of thinking. Let's take a closer look at the four developmental tasks that couples undertake in the reconciliation stage.

1. Clarify Your Sense of Self

In order to fully embrace your role in the relationship, you need to have a clear understanding of who you are. Personal growth is a vital life-affirming process. As humorist Frank Gelett Burgess notes, "If in the last few years you haven't discarded a major opinion or acquired a new one, check your pulse. You may be dead."

As you've worked through your unresolved issues from the past, you've no doubt uncovered some aspects of your self that might be undesirable or unnerving. The good news is that you don't have to carry those experiences around like hand-me-downs for the rest of your life. As an individual, you have an incredible capacity to live a whole and fulfilling life.

In *The Search for the Real Self*, Dr. James Masterson outlines the potential that each person has to:

- experience a wide range of feelings deeply;
- expect that life can be mastered and good things achieved;
- be assertive and take steps toward their wishes, dreams, and goals;
- acknowledge their self esteem and self worth;
- soothe painful feelings;
- make and stick to commitments;
- express creativity;
- experience intimacy;
- accommodate and enjoy being alone;
- recognize and sustain their inner feelings, perceptions, values, and beliefs.[1]

If you are already able to do each of these things, you're probably living a remarkable life. If you're just beginning to explore your sense of self, any one of these ten areas is a great place to start. Because you always have the opportunity to explore new ideas and activities, the process of self discovery is one that can inspire you at any point in life. Consider celebrated American folk artist Grandma Moses. She didn't discover her love of painting until she was seventy-five years old, but she painted 1,600 pieces before her death at the age of 101.

What inspires you? What motivates you? What are you passionate about? The answers to these questions are a great jumpstart on your way to deepening your sense of self. When you are fully confident in who you are, you have a much greater capacity to love others. After all, you cannot give away what you do not yourself possess.

2. Embrace Independence

When couples first form a relationship, their intense romantic fantasies and flurry of activity to merge two separate lives into one relationship often result in dependence. It isn't until you have truly worked through your broken expectations and power struggles that you can understand the freedom of independence.

It's difficult to describe a set of steps or activities that if followed lead to independence. Rather, becoming your own person is a process. It does, however, require that you and your partner once again expand the boundaries of your relationship to accept that you will never think, believe, and act in exactly the same ways. For example, one of you may always vote Democrat, and the other might always vote Republican. One may always fill the car up with gas when the needle hits a quarter of a tank, but the other might always let the needle bounce around empty. Or one may always support the arts while the other might think that art is a waste of time.

The point is that, at some point, you must agree to disagree. This doesn't mean that you reach a stalemate and stop talking while clinging to feelings of anger or resentment. It means that both you and your partner accept the fact that you disagree, but you continue to love and accept each other as individuals. You fight the battles that need fighting, and for the rest of it you move on. Perhaps Reinhold Niebuhr said it best in the first portion of his now-famous Serenity Prayer:

> God grant me the serenity
> to accept the things I cannot change;

courage to change the things I can;
and wisdom to know the difference.

3. Take and Share Responsibility

A significant portion of this book focuses on the past: your separation-individuation process, your parents' marriage, and the beliefs and behaviors from your family of origin. But that doesn't give you license to live in the past. In order to be truly independent within your relationship, both you and your partner must take responsibility for your own thoughts, feelings, and behaviors. If you carry any resentment or blame toward your partner and use it as an excuse for your own behavior, you have not fully reconciled your relationship.

All of this independence talk might inspire a few Lone Ranger fantasies, but taking responsibility for self-fulfillment doesn't mean that you abandon or ignore your partner. While you're free to be yourself, that freedom still exists within the boundaries of your marriage. Therefore, it comes with the responsibility to share in the activities of daily life, applauding each other's strengths and encouraging each other in your limitations. It also means being sexually and emotionally faithful to each other and to the commitment that you have made to your relationship.

*   *   *

Marriage Tool #5: Forgiveness

While communication, problem-solving, conflict-resolution, and negotiation skills primarily pertain to how we think, forgiveness is a matter of the heart. If you cling to bitterness, anger, hostility, hatred, resentment, or a fear of being hurt or humiliated, you will not only destroy your relationship, but you'll also destroy yourself.

Forgiveness is possibly the most powerful conscious act in the human experience. It has the unparalleled power to bridge the chasm between two wounded people and break the cycle of accusation and pain. And yet, while forgiveness weaves its way through every major world religion and has been practiced for untold thousands of years, it's something that we're only now beginning to understand. The art of forgiveness is one of the hottest fields in clinical psychology today, with over 1,200 published studies, up from 58 in 1997.[2] The most widely studied topic is forgiveness in marriage relationships.

A national Gallup poll indicates that 94 percent of Americans surveyed said it was important to forgive, but only 48 percent said that they usually tried to forgive others.[3] So what makes forgiveness so difficult? Some say that it is a sign of weakness, that by offering forgiveness we become codependent doormats, excusing or accepting the hurtful behavior of others. Others argue that it's a gift given only to the very spiritual and cannot be learned. I am one of the many people who disagree on both accounts.

Not only is forgiveness not a sign of weakness, it is a proclamation of strength. It gives you the opportunity to chart the course of your own thoughts and feelings rather than merely reacting to the behavior of others. Forgiveness does not condone another person's behavior or sweep the consequences of that behavior under the rug. It simply releases you from a self-imposed obligation of anger and bitterness by letting go of your own suffering.

Forgiveness is also a learned skill, not a momentary response. It is your key to freedom from the past. If you put your energy into your memories of being wronged, you'll never be able to reconcile with the one who wronged you.

One of the best explanations on how to forgive comes from Dr. Frederic Luskin, who outlines the process in the following nine steps:

- Know exactly how you feel about what happened and why it's not okay.
- Make a commitment to do what you have to do to feel better. Forgiveness is for you and no one else. No one else even has to know about your decision.
- Understand your goal. Forgiveness doesn't always mean reconciliation. It can also be the "peace and understanding that come from blaming that which has hurt you less, taking the life experience less personally, and changing your grievance story."
- Get the right perspective. Recognize that your real pain comes from the hurt feelings, thoughts, and physical upset you are suffering now, not what hurt you two minutes or ten years ago.
- Practice simple stress-management techniques to soothe your body's flight-or-fight response.
- Give up your expectations. You cannot expect things from other people, or your life, that they do not choose to give you. You can hope for health, love, friendship, and prosperity and work hard to get them, but if you demand these things when you don't have the power to make them happen, you're the one who suffers.

- Redirect your energy. Look for another way to meet your goals rather than through the experience that has hurt you. Instead of mentally replaying your hurt, look for new ways to get what you want.

- Remember that a life well lived is your best revenge. Instead of focusing on your wounded feelings and giving power over you to the person who caused you pain, learn to look for the love, beauty, and kindness around you.

- Change your grievance story to remind you of the heroic choice to forgive.[4]

Perhaps the most common misconception about forgiveness is the idea of forgiving and forgetting. In truth, you should never forget the grievance but change how you remember it. When you reconcile your relationship, you are able to remember the event as a step toward cultivating a more emotionally, spiritually, and physically intimate and compassionate relationship.

*   *   *

4. Cultivate a Deeper Intimacy

Intimacy in the reconciliation stage differs from the intimacy of the honeymoon stage. It focuses less on sexual activity and more on the art of friendship. It is a genuine desire to spend time in each other's company. In defining the true test of friendship, author Eugene Kennedy asks:

> Can you literally do nothing without the other person? Can you enjoy together those moments of life that are utterly simple? They are the moments people look back on at the end of life and number as their most sacred experiences.

This sense of mutual friendship comes from caring as much about your partner's well-being as your own, while still knowing that you are separate beings. You are not totally dependent or independent. You are interdependent. Where dependence is being influenced or controlled by another person, and independence is a complete lack of influence or control by others, interdependence is a mutual relationship in which partners thrive better together than on their own. They are free to be themselves, and yet they choose to be together.

One of my favorite ways to encourage people in this task is to have them select a favorite picture of their partner—not just the perfunctory family picture on the desk at the office, but a photograph that truly captures what they love about that person. Every time they look at that picture (and I recommend doing so frequently), I ask them to create a mental list of the simple pleasures that they share with their partner—their scent, their smile, the sound of their voice, the feel of their skin. When you literally surround yourself with thoughts and images of your lover, you cannot help but grow to love him or her more.

Getting Stuck

It's difficult to get stuck in the reconciliation stage because reconciliation is an active process. You either choose to participate or not. Usually, when a couple is unable to reconcile their individual wants and needs within the marriage, it's because they are also stuck in a previous stage or past experience. If you find yourself in this position, I recommend that you go back to the stage that truly resonates with your present situation and rework the unfinished developmental tasks required to move forward. This is also a good time to seek guidance from a marriage and family therapist or a trusted pastor, counselor, or advisor.

Do Try This at Home: The Art of Forgiveness

To practice the art of forgiveness, take some time away from your partner to answer the following questions. When you begin to forgive other people, I recommend that you start by focusing on one person or even on one particular issue pertaining to that person.

1. How do I feel about the event/issue? Are my thoughts and feelings about this event/issue tied to other thoughts, feelings, memories, or experiences?

    _____

    _____

    _____

    _____

2. How might the other person feel about the event/issue?

    _____

_____

_____

_____

3. Why is the event/issue a problem for me?

_____

_____

_____

4. Did I do anything to contribute to the situation?

_____

_____

_____

5. Am I clinging to any unrealistic expectations regarding this event/issue?

_____

_____

_____

6. What do I hope to achieve by forgiving this person? What do I need in order to be at peace? What will change when I've achieved it?

_____

_____

_____

_____

7.   How can I meet my goals without traveling down this path again?

_____

_____

_____

_____

When you are able to forgive your partner for past wounds, you will be able to view those experiences less personally, take responsibility for your own thoughts and feelings, and reshape the relationship to grow and prosper as an individual and as part of a couple.

Moving On

When couples are able to use conflict and disagreements as opportunities to learn something about themselves; when they see their differences as an enhancement and not a threat to their relationship; when they fully recognize and accept their interdependence, they have achieved acceptance.

Stage Six: Acceptance ~ The Legacy of Love

New love is brightest, and long love is greatest;
but revived love is the tenderest thing known upon earth.
~ Thomas Hardy
(*The Hand of Ethelberta*)

Acceptance, the sixth stage of marriage, is the culmination of everything that a couple has worked toward through the five previous stages. Although it shares many of its emotions and activities with reconciliation, it takes the relationship one step further. While couples in the reconciliation stage are still striving to develop a sense of self and create interdependence within the relationship, these aspects come more naturally for couples in the stage of acceptance.

Husbands and wives who accept each other agree to receive what their partners bring to their relationships without judgment or retaliation. They have favorable opinions of one another and regard their relationships as both right and true. They have long ago ceased to pretend to be people they are not just to please their partners. Instead, they have learned that by being themselves they are most free to love someone else. In these relationships, partners are fully accepted and fully accepting of each other.

Acceptance is not a utopia of candlelit dinners and rose petals. I don't know of any couples who don't continue to rework and resolve conflict throughout the course of their lives. But with skillful use of communication, problem solving, conflict resolution, and negotiation, accepting couples can express anger, frustration, and disappointment without threatening their partners or their relationships.

With less attention focused on restoring the relationship, Acceptance also ushers in a time of surging personal growth. Instead of pouring so much energy into their marriages, couples who are secure in their love are free to explore new ways of fulfilling their creative, intellectual, artistic, professional, or spiritual passions—passions that might have been overlooked in earlier years. For many, this period of intense love and passion marks the best years of the relationship.

116

Couples who successfully achieve reconciliation and acceptance experience a tender and intimate love unparalleled in any other stage.

They enjoy storge love and the warmth and comfort of simply being together. As individuals, they are not as new or polished as they once were, but they dearly love each other's worn edges and rich patina of familiarity.

And let's not forget about eros love, the passionate, dizzying, and desirous love of being "in love." Lovers who are fully accepted and fully accepting of each other share an enduring emotional and physical bond that stirs the heart, even after the first flavors of divine madness ebb away.

Perhaps the most rewarding love of acceptance, however, is that of philia, or friendship. Friendship isn't accidental or easy. It doesn't just land in our laps. True friendship can only bloom between two people who are confident in themselves and wish to share in the joys and sorrows of life. Friendship isn't love by instinct; it's love by choice. Partners who weather life's storms together build a deep and enduring bond of friendship that grows beyond affection or romance. They truly value each other.

Accepting couples—those who have reconciled their broken expectations and power struggles, those who have found themselves within their relationships—are also the people most able to embrace agape love. Knowing that they themselves are deeply loved and cared for, they focus their desire on what is best for their beloved. They love unconditionally, desiring only the best for each other. Again, this love is a choice. While storge and eros are fueled by proximity or passion, agape comes from a transformation of the heart. When couples can lay everything on the line and expect nothing in return, they achieve love in its highest, truest form.

When we fall in love, the bliss of early romance lays the foundation for the reservoir of powerful emotion that sustains us through the dry and distant periods. As that love matures, we also have the capacity to fill that reservoir with deep feelings of love, care, responsibility, and respect. And that love, care, responsibility, and respect is what we pass on to the generations that follow.

*   *   *

Marriage Tool #6: Maintaining a Reservoir of Love and Respect

Have you ever thought about how we take pictures? If you flip through most people's photo albums, you'll find pictures of birthday parties and Christmas mornings, graduations and anniversaries, and lots of "first" experiences: first bath, first haircut, first homerun, first piano recital, first dance. Instinctively, we tell people to smile before we capture a moment forever. We all know that life isn't really a series of celebrations, and yet we rarely take pictures of illness, accidents, tension, arguments, break ups, job loss, or death. When we look back on our lives, we choose to remember the good things, the days that brought us laughter and joy. We need to do the same for our marriages.

By snapping mental pictures of your partner's gifts, talents, skills, and positive characteristics, you begin to build a reservoir of love and respect that will encourage you through the rocky patches of your relationship. Each time you remember why you fell in love in the first place, capture that moment and that feeling.

Or go one step further and write it down. I know of a couple who started a bedtime notebook to do just that. Each night before bed, one partner writes something to the other and leaves the notebook under the partner's pillow. The notes often include little lists of things they appreciate or love about the other person. Sometimes they are silly, sometimes serious, but they are always encouraging and appreciated. The next night, the opposite partner responds with a note and returns the notebook. What a great tool this is for building a reservoir. When this couple struggles or argues, they have a very long list of self-proclaimed affirmations recorded in their notebook to remind them about the love and respect that sustains their relationship.

Continue to carve out time for each other. Spend fifteen to thirty minutes of uninterrupted time together each day. Create special dating experiences to recapture the early bliss of love, and take mini-breaks away from family and friends every few months to refresh your relationship. Love is organic, and like all living things it must be cultivated and nurtured, or it will die.

*   *   *

Do Try This at Home: Building a Reservoir

To begin building a reservoir of love, take some time away from your partner to answer the following questions. While your answers should be honest, they don't need to be profound. In many cases, it's the little things in life that end up meaning the most.

1.   What three characteristics first attracted you to your partner?

_____

_____

_____

2. What three things do you admire about your partner?

_____

_____

_____

3. What are your three favorite physical attributes about your partner?

_____

_____

_____

4. When you think about your partner, what three things are you proud of?

_____

_____

_____

5. What three things does your partner do for you that make you feel loved?

_____

_____

_____

6. What is your favorite memory of your partner?

_____

_____

7. What is your favorite thing to do together with your partner?

    _____

    _____

    _____

8. What does your partner do better than anyone else?

    _____

    _____

    _____

9. When you think about your partner, what three words come to mind?

    _____

    _____

    _____

10. When your partner is absent, what three things about him/her do you miss the most?

    _____

    _____

    _____

When you've both answered these questions, plan a specific activity to do together where you will share your answers with each other. It could be as simple as a Starbucks coffee date or as elaborate as a weekend getaway. The goal is to begin creating moments that will become lasting memories.

Leaving a Legacy of Love

The very fact that you've picked up a marriage book says something about you. You want to leave a better legacy of love than the one you're currently living. The fact that you've made it to the last chapter indicates that you're serious.

Many of the tasks that you've tackled throughout the chapters of this book focus on your past: your childhood, your family, and your parents' marriage. Just as those relationships and experiences from your past impact your current relationship, your current relationship will impact the future relationships of your children.

Hundreds of books about marriage and parenting have been written and will be written in the years to come. But many of them would be unnecessary if we could restore relationships between husbands and wives. There is no greater gift that parents can give their children than to first and foremost love each other. As author James Baldwin wrote, "Children have never been very good at listening to their elders, but they have never failed to imitate them."

Thus, you are faced with a life-changing choice. Will you leave for your children a legacy of broken expectations, power struggles, restlessness, and pain? Or will you leave a legacy of love, care, responsibility, respect, and knowledge?[1] These five elements work together to create a powerful legacy of love. Love is an active process. It is in giving that we love, not in receiving. If we cannot love, then we cannot care for care is the active concern for the life and growth of that which we love. And if we do not care for someone, then we do not voluntarily respond to the needs of others. Yet even if we could respond, responsibility without knowledge is blind to need, and without knowing someone, we cannot offer respect—to see someone as they are and allow them to grow in his or her own way for his or her own benefit and not for the purpose of meeting our needs.

These five actions, when woven together, create the fabric of our marriages, or, as Anne Morrow Lindbergh describes, "a web that is taut and firm."

> The web is fashioned of love. Yes, but many kinds of love: romantic love first, then a slow-growing devotion, and playing through these, a constantly rippling companionship. It is made of loyalties, and interdependencies, and shared experiences. It is woven of memories of meetings and conflicts; of triumphs and disappointments. It is a web of communication, a common language, and the acceptance of lack of language, too; a knowledge of likes and dislikes, of habits and reactions, both physical and mental. It is a web of instincts and intuitions, and known and unknown exchanges. The web of marriage is made

by propinquity, in the day to day living side by side, looking outward and working outward in the same direction. It is woven in space and in time of the substance of life itself.[2]

May your marriage journey bring you joy.

About the Author

Liberty Kovacs, PhD, is a marriage and family therapist with over forty years of professional experience as an educator, consultant, and marriage and family therapist. She specializes in couple relationships and developmental transitions over time. Her work with nearly 2,400 couples has seen overwhelmingly positive responses.

Dr. Kovacs holds a doctorate in marriage and family therapy from California Graduate School of Family Psychology and a master's degree in psychiatric nursing from the University of California at San Francisco. She received her California state license as a marriage, family, and child counselor in 1967.

Her published works include contributions to *I Want A Baby, He Doesn't: How Both Partners Can Make The Right Decision At The Right Time* (2005) by Donna Wade, *The Therapist's Notebook: Homework, Handouts and Activities for use in Psychotherapy* (1998) by. L.L. Hecker, and *When One Partner is Willing and the Other is Not* (1997) edited by Barbara Jo Brothers, as well as articles in *Journal of Couples Therapy*. (2000, 1997, 1994), *Body & Soul* (1993), *Family Therapy* (1988, 1983), *The Sacramento Union* (1987), and *Marriage & Divorce Today Newsletter* (1986).

Dr. Kovacs is the mother of three adult sons and has two grandchildren who light up her life. She lives in Sacramento, California, where she loves to read, write, and garden. Dr. Kovacs is actively involved in her church and several peace promoting social groups as well as the Network for Spiritual Progressives and Therapists for Social Responsibility.

Dr. Kovacs produced a video tape in 1989 called, *Today's Marriage. The Six Stages.* Hara Estroff Marano interviewed her for the article, "The Reinvention of Marriage. The New Couple Research Can Save Your Marriage—Before it Starts" which was published in *Psychology Today*, Jan./Feb 1992. Other therapists and researchers mentioned in the article were: Florence Kaslow, Ph.D., Howard Markman, John Gottman, Elizabeth M. Douvan, professor of psychology and research scientist.

Dr. Kovacs contributed material on marital development to: Mary Kirk who wrote *The Marriage Workout Book: A Marriage Care Book* published in 1996 by Lion Publishing, Oxford, England and Albatross Books in Sutherland, Australia.

My Memoirs, Liberty's Quest … is due to be published in the Spring, 2008 by Robert D. Reed Publishers, Bandon, Oregon.

	Honeymoon	Expectation	Power Struggle	Seven-Year Itch	Reconciliation	Acceptance
Stage	Honeymoon	Expectation	Power Struggle	Seven-Year Itch	Reconciliation	Acceptance
Theme	Free love	Compromise	Control	Competition	Cooperation	Collaboration
Tasks	Nurture each other. Develop a basis for satisfactory sex and a caring, supportive relationship. Develop sense of belonging.	Relinquish family of origin. Establish firm boundaries and self-esteem.	Begin developing problem-solving, decision-making, and negotiating procedures. Learn responsibility for own thoughts, feelings, and actions. Support partner's growth as an individual	Develop individually, and see partner as a separate person	Develop a clearer sense of self. Understand that the strivings for independence are normal. Take responsibility for individual needs. Develop a more open, honest approach with partner directly leading to increased intimacy.	Stabilize perspective of self and partner. Choose to stay in relationship. Take responsibility for satisfying own needs. Support partner's strengths and successes.
Attitudes	"We are one. We are the same. I need you." Partners give and receive with no effort.	"You are changing. You are different. You hurt me. You are not living up to my expectations."	"If you won't be like me, I'll leave you."	"Who am I? Can I make it without him/her? I want to be me."	"I am beginning to recognize my own inner struggles."	"I am seeing you as you are." Partners enjoy themselves and enjoy being together.
Affective Tone	Passionate, romantic, infatuated, madly in love, lots of eye contact and touching	Disappointment, anxiety, conformity, accommodation, wanting to be close but not knowing how to reach each other	Ambivalence, distrust, anger, blaming, polarization, confrontation	Fight/flight, argumentative, withdrawal	Reconciliation, seeing self/other as a real live separate person who may not meet one's own	Accepting, high levels of warmth
Expectations	"You will provide for my needs, wants, and happiness."	"You must make me happy." Closeness and dependence may give way to the reality of household tasks.	"Why won't you make me happy?" Each partner has definite opinions about the way their partner should be. Each is afraid of giving in to the other. "She's manipulative." "He won't see my position has validity."	"I can make myself happy. I can take care of myself. I need some time/space for myself."	Expectations, acceptance of the parts of self that create such expectations	"I'll take care of my needs and wants, and you'll take care of yours."

Marriage—A User's Guide

Perceptions	"You are perfect. You are mine. I am yours."	"You are changing. What's wrong with me?"	"You are just like my mother/father. You don't love me. You are selfish, self-centered."	"I love myself."	"You have your conflicts, and I have mine. I can't change you, and you can't change me."	"We can be separate and we can reconnect without losing our identities." A time of surging personal growth, no need to pour energy into saving marriage.
Problems	If one partner moves faster toward independence in providing for him/herself with job or friends, he/she may be pulled back by the other, who may feel devastated that their partner wants to do something with someone else.	Problems may arise when partners are on different timetables in realizing they don't have to do everything together or feel the same at all times. One partner may feel rejected. Couple must work out how to be apart and still enjoy activities together. They must begin to find ways to reconcile their differences.	Power struggle can be intense. Partners get stuck in patterns of accusation and blame. "You always forget to ..." Both partners feel pain and distress.	Struggle for independence marks major change in marital relations. Some relationships will survive separation or end in divorce at this time. One or both partners may begin distancing self from partner with an affair, turning outward and searching environment for partners rather than turning inward and completing self-identity process.	Couple struggles toward intimacy. Partner may uncover unresolved conflicts from family of origin.	Conflicts are handled as they arise through negotiation.
Transitions	Partners begin to recognize that they are not exactly alike.	Recognition and affirmation of differences.	Recognition of need to control. Begin taking independent or autonomous positions. Couple takes little steps to reconnect; they talk more. They make an effort to understand and try to acknowledge what the other is feeling.	Recognition that each has individual needs to resolve. Recognition of own limitations. Stating wants/needs more openly. Can maintain one's own identity in the relationship. Partner chooses to resolves issue of independence within the relationship.	Use of conflicts and disagreements as opportunities for learning about selves. See differences as enhancement of relationship rather than threat. Ups and downs are increasingly predictable.	Recognition and acceptance of interdependence.

			"I know you're feeling hurt but" One partner may realize patterns tap into struggles with parents that were never resolved.			

Notes

1. Love and Other Difficulties

1   Robert Johnson, *The Fisher King and the Handless Maiden: Understanding the Wounded Feeling Function in Masculine and Feminine Psychology* (New York: Harper San Francisco, 1993), 6.

2   Merriam Webster Online Dictionary (http://www.merriam-webster.com/cgi-bin/dictionary)

3   C. S. Lewis, *The Four Loves* (New York: Harcourt Brace & Company, 1960), 34.

4   Jerome Travers, "Love and Marriage and Other Silly Delusions," *Journal of Couples Therapy*, vol. 2, #3 (1991), 85.

5   Jerome Travers, "Love and Marriage and Other Silly Delusions," *Journal of Couples Therapy*, vol. 2 #3 (1991), 86.

6   John A. Desteian, *Coming Together—Coming Apart: The Union of Opposites in Love Relationships.* (Boston: SIGO Press, 1989), 62.

7   Excerpt from THE FOUR LOVES, copyright © C. S. Lewis, 1960, renewed 1988 by Arthur Owen Barfield, reprinted by permission of Harcourt, Inc.

8   M. Scott Peck, *The Road Less Traveled: A New Psychology of Love, Traditional Values and Spiritual Growth* (New York: Simon & Schuster, 25th ann. ed., 2002), 81.

9   Marilyn Yalom, *A History of the Wife* (New York: HarperCollins, 2001), 320.

10 Steven Mintz and Susan Kellogg, *Domestic Revolutions* (New York: Free Press, 1988), 171.

11 Marilyn Yalom, *A History of the Wife* (New York: HarperCollins, 2001), xvii.

12 Gerald I. Manus, "Marriage counseling: a technique in search of theory," *Journal of Marriage and the Family*, vol. 28 (1966): 449–453.

2. No Man is an Island

1   www.brainyquote.com.

2   Caroline Geuzaine, Marianne Debry, and Vinciane Liesens, "Separation from parents in late adolescence: The same for boys and girls?" *Journal of Youth & Adolescence, 29* (2000), 79–91.

3   Martin Grotjahn, *Dynamics of Growth and Maturation in Marriage and Psychoanalysis*, printed in Salo Rosenbaum and Ian Alger (eds.), *The Marriage Relationship: Psychoanalytic Perspectives* (New York: Basic Books, 1969), 344 & 349.

4   Louise J. Kaplan, *Oneness and Separateness* (New York: Simon and Schuster, 1978), 31.

3. The Apple Doesn't Fall Far From the Tree

1   Marg Stark, *What No One Tells the Bride: Surviving the Wedding, Sex after the Honeymoon, Second Thoughts, Wedding Cake Freezer Burn, Becoming Your Mother, Screaming about In-Laws, Maintaining your Identity, and Being Blissfully Happy Despite it All* (New York: Hyperion, 1998), 134–135.

2   Gary Chapman, *The Five Love Languages: How to Express Heartfelt Commitment to Your Mate* (Chicago: Northfield Publishing, 1992), 37.

3   William Shakespeare, *As You Like It*, Act II, Scene VII (1598–1599)

4   Arlie Hochschild, *The Second Shift: Working Parents and the Revolution at Home* (New York: Viking, 1989), 304.

4. Assumptions Are Deadly!

1   Patricia Farrell, *How to be Your Own Therapist: A Step-by-Step Guide to Building a Competent, Confident Life* (New York: McGraw-Hill, 2003), 155.

2   Leo Tolstoy, *Anna Karenina*, translated by David Magarshack (New York: Signet Classics, 1961), 17.

3   Monica McGoldrick and Randy Gerson, *Genograms in Family Assessment* (New York: W. W. Norton & Company, 1985), 1.

4   Patricia Farrell, *How to be Your Own Therapist: A Step-by-Step Guide to Building a Competent, Confident Life* (New York: McGraw-Hill, 2003), 156.

5. Mapping A Marriage

1   Paul Reiser, *Couplehood* (New York: Bantam Books, 1994), 207–209.

2   Joseph Barth, *Ladies Home Journal* (1961, April).

3   Roger L. Gould, *Transformations: Growth and Change in Adult Life* (New York: Simon and Schuster, 1978), 279.

4   Evelyn M. Duvall, *Family Development* (New York: J.P. Lippincott & Co., 1957), 31–33.

5   Rainer Maria Rilke, *Letters to a Young Poet* (New York: Random House, 1984), 68.

6. Stage One: The Honeymooners

1   Merriam Webster Online Diction ary (<u>http://www.merrian-webster.com/cgi-bin/dictionary</u>)

2   Virginia Satir, *Conjoint family therapy. A guide to theory and technique* (Palo Alto, Ca: Science and Behavior Books, Inc., 1964), 155.

3   Howard Markman, Scott Stanley, and Susan L. Blumberg, *Fighting for Your Marriage* (San Francisco: Jossey-Bass Publishers, 1994), 49.

4   John Durham Peters, *Speaking Into the Air: A History of the Idea of Communication* (Chicago, IL: University of Chicago Press, 1999), 7.

5   Merriam Webster Online Dictionary (<u>http://www.merriam-webster.com/cgi-bin/dictionary</u>)

6   Stephen Arterburn and Fred Stoeker, *Every Woman's Desire: Every Man's Guide to Winning the Heart of a Woman* (Colorado Springs, CO: Waterbrook Press, 2001), 61.

7   Taken from *My Soul Thirsts: An Invitation to Intimacy with God* by Steve Korch. Copyright ©2000 by Judson Press. Used by permission of Judson Press. wwwjudsonpress.com.

8   From GIFTS FROM THE SEA by Anne Morrow Lindbergh, copyright © 1955, 1975, renewed 1983 by Anne Morrow Lindbergh. Used by permission of Pantheon Books, a division of Random House, Inc.

9   Maxine Rock, *The Marriage Map: Understanding and Surviving the Stages of Marriage* (Atlanta: Peachtree Publishers, Ltd., 1986), 23.

8. Stage Three: The Power Struggle

1   Rollo May, *Power and Innocence: A Search for the Sources of Violence* (New York: W. W. Norton and Co., 1998), 20.

2   Merriam Webster Online Dictionary (<u>http://www.merriam-webster.com/cgi-bin/dictionary</u>)

3   James S. Hewett, *Illustrations Unlimited* (Wheaton, Illinois: Tyndale House Publishers, Inc., 1988), 332.

4   John Gottman, *Why Marriages Succeed or Fail: And How to Make Yours Last* (New York: Simon & Schuster, 1994), 28.

5   Joseph Luft, *Group Processes: An Introduction to Group Dynamics* (Palo Alto, CA: The National Press, 1963), 10.

6   Rainer Maria Rilke, *Rilke on Love and Other Difficulties* (New York: W. W. Norton and Co., 1993), 28.

9. Stage Four: The Seven-Year Itch

[1] From THE PROPHET by Kahlil Gibran, copyright 1923 by Kahlil Gibran and renewed 1951 by Administrators C.T.A. of Kahlil Gibran Estate and Mary G. Gibran. Used by permission of Alfred A. Knopf, a division of Random House, Inc.

[2] Max Bazerman, *Judgment in Managerial Decision Making* (New York: Wiley, 1986).

[3] Ellyn Bader and Peter T. Pearson, *In Quest of the Mythical Mate: A Development Approach to Diagnosis and Treatment in Couples Therapy* (New York: Brunner/Mazel Publishers, 1988), 205.

10. Stage Five: Reconciliation ~ Viva la Difference!

[1] James F. Masterson, *The Search for the Real Self: Unmasking the Personality Disorders of our Age* (New York: Free Press, 1988), 42-46.

[2] Jordana Lewis and Jerry Adler, "Forgive and Let Live; Revenge Is Sweet, but Letting Go of Anger at Those Who Wronged You Is a Smart Route to Good Health," *Newsweek* (2004, September 27), 54.

[3] The Campaign for Forgiveness Research (http://www.forgiving.org).

[4] Frederic Luskin, *Forgive for Good* (New York: HarperCollins, 2002), 211-212.

11. Stage Six: Acceptance ~ The Legacy of Love

[1] Erich Fromm, *The Art of Loving* (New York: Harper, 1956), 22–26.

[2] From GIFTS FROM THE SEA by Anne Morrow Lindbergh, copyright © 1955, 1975, renewed 1983 by Anne Morrow Lindbergh. Used by permission of Pantheon Books, a division of Random House, Inc.

978-0-595-40709-5
0-595-40709-9

Printed in the United States
117795LV00004BA/273/A

9 780595 407095